Urban Mammals

a concise guide

Whittet Books Ltd
1 St John's Lane
Stansted
Essex CM24 8JU
Email: mail@whittetbooks.com

First published 2012
Text © People's Trust for Endangered Species 2012
See page 103 for photograph and illustration copyright
details.

A catalogue record for this publication is available from the
British Library.

ISBN 978 1 873580 85 1

Designed by Lodge Graphics

Urban Mammals

a concise guide

David Wembridge

Editor: Jill Nelson
Picture Editor: Zoe Roden

Whittet Books

Contents

Foreword

We all daydream of pristine wilderness areas undamaged by the heavy hand of man where animals survive in dynamic harmony and in abundances which would shock us – all in a landscape which would define natural beauty. And then most of us wake up to the urban world where we have made a manscape very alien from nature.

But for me there is a true and rich beauty here too, where natural perfection is highlighted through its framing amongst our chaos. The contrast is striking and serves to exaggerate the two worlds drawn together by our on-going and ever-changing impacts. What is also uplifting is nature's tenacity, its determination to succeed in spite of us, to seek out a niche which is close enough to its original that it not only survives but prospers. And that because so many of us live in this modified environment it is also the place where we are most likely to meet and engage with this guild of animals. In fact, meeting them is sometimes actually far easier simply because they have grown accustomed to living amongst us and for many people these encounters can be formative and thus important.

Many species have crossed the line and moved into our world: plants, birds, insects and, of course, mammals, and some of these have made themselves very obviously at home. Last week I had a superb encounter with a stunning and friendly fox at the bottom of my father's driveway. Yesterday evening I saw four roe deer nibbling the verge of the M8 right in the heart of Glasgow but this morning I passed the corpse of a badger driving into Southampton – proving that despite success there are always setbacks when wildlife tries to adapt to our 'progress'. Sadder still is that I cannot now remember when I last saw an urban hedgehog; these affable favourites seem to have disappeared.

I hope that this introduction to Britain's urban mammal fauna will lead to a real appreciation of its fragility, its beauty and its real value, that intolerance and prejudice will be banished and that, like me, you will celebrate and enjoy this remarkable set of creatures.

Chris Packham

Introduction

Urban living

Urban areas cover between two and three per cent of the world's land area and are home to an ever-increasing proportion of the human population. Since 2008, over half of people globally have lived in urban areas and, by the middle of the century, it is forecast that 70 per cent of us will be urbanites.

In the UK, built land makes up almost a tenth of the land area and is home to four-fifths of us; it is here – in the green spaces and the brick and concrete habitats of our towns and cities – that most of us encounter wildlife from day to day.

Eighty per cent of the UK's population live in urban areas.

In England and Wales, 'urban' is used by the Office for National Statistics to describe settlements with more than 10,000 inhabitants; elsewhere, other criteria are used and worldwide, the term 'urban' encompasses very different types of settlement. In this book, 'urban' is used less strictly than in its official sense to refer to the built environment, including towns and villages that might be made up of only a few dozen houses and other buildings. As such, it encompasses an even greater number of us.

But whether they are classified as urban or not, towns provide habitats for wildlife and there are no neat boundaries between built and natural landscapes – wherever you are, nature will move in, unbothered by definitions. Towns and cities, large or small, concentrate food, produce warmth and waste, and bring together communities of species (intentionally or accidentally) that are found nowhere else. In 2010, Jennifer Owen described the findings of a thirty-year study of her own medium-sized suburban garden in Leicester. She recorded 2,673 species of cultivated and wild plants and animals in a plot 61 metres long by 15 metres wide, including 20 that no-one had ever spotted in Britain before and four that were entirely new to science. Seven were wild mammal species (of the 55 or so mammal species resident in Great Britain and Ireland, not counting whales and dolphins) and nationwide, three times as many mammal species can be found in gardens and urban green spaces.

Since it began in 2003, People's Trust for Endangered Species' *Living with Mammals* survey has collected records of mammals in the built environment – spaces such as gardens, allotments, cemeteries and civic parks, as well as sites adjacent to more rural buildings. Over 24 species have been recorded, including some, such as otters, hedgehogs, pipistrelle bats and red squirrels, that are the focus of conservation efforts in Britain.

Not all mammals are as urbanite as others: rodents – such as wood and house mice, and brown and black rats – have lived beside us for millennia; others have moved in only more recently. Foxes are urban-dwellers *par excellence*, along with red and grey squirrels that readily make use of parks and gardens. Bat species, pine martens and edible dormice too will take the opportunity to roost or den in roof spaces, and roe and muntjac deer will take advantage of rich pickings in gardens and allotments.

What is it that makes one species more suited to urban life than another? A study of birds in the city of Jerusalem found that being successful in highly-urbanised environments depended not on brain size, or how good a species was at adapting to new situations, but on a combination of more mundane traits: diet, how sedentary and social a species is, and the type of nest sites it prefers. If the same is true for mammals, then by providing good foraging and nesting sites, we might encourage more to move in.

Most modern gardens are not as large as Jennifer Owen's, but size (and whether a garden is more or less urban) is not as critical as some other features. One thing that is important (from studies such as the BUGS projects, run by the University of Sheffield) seems to be trees: for small mammals and insects at least, tall vegetation is more important than how built-up the area is in determining abundance. And there is evidence too that the actions of gardeners – such as building a log pile or growing plants bearing fruits, nuts or seed-cones – can make a difference to urban mammals. The findings of *Living with Mammals* suggest that sites that produced berries or seeds, or that had a shed, pond or woodpile, were associated with a greater abundance of species. Similarly, a study by Phil Baker and Stephen Harris of residential gardens in Bristol found that an increase in the number of wildlife-friendly habitats in a garden and/or the number of food-bearing plants was associated with an increase in the proportion of gardens frequently used by hedgehogs and mice – and, for hedgehogs at least, whose numbers nationally have fallen by a quarter in the last ten years, that might just be a saving grace.

The value of green spaces

The idea that the environment and biodiversity have tangible benefits – that they provide what are called 'ecosystem services' – is one that is talked about more and more, and the green spaces in towns and cities are no exception. Both individually and socially, we benefit from them: we use parks and recreational spaces to play and exercise, and gardens and allotments to grow food; and they have environmental benefits, helping to prevent surface-water flooding and keeping cities cool. The biodiversity that they support, too, is valuable: trees improve air quality by absorbing emissions and reduce noise levels; insects, such as bees and moths, pollinate flowers and crops such as fruit trees and tomato plants; and natural predators, from hoverflies to hedgehogs, control pest species. Moreover, contact with natural spaces makes us feel good. As well as providing environmental benefits, experiencing wildlife in gardens and parks has measurable physical and mental benefits – we recover from illness more quickly and feel happier – and the greater the diversity of species, the greater are the benefits. When it comes down to hard-nosed economics, the monetary value of the health benefit of living with a view of green spaces was estimated in the UK National Ecosystem Assessment in 2011 to be £300 per person every year.

An urban patchwork

Urban landscapes are patchy and most mammals, unlike birds, encounter the obstacles of roads and fences when moving about. Thinking 'bigger' – linking-up green spaces and acting on a neighbourhood-scale for wildlife rather than that of a single garden – is necessary when we consider that the home ranges of mammals are usually much bigger than a single garden or park.

Different types of semi-natural habitats make up the urban patchwork, including gardens, parks, playing fields, railway embankments, derelict ground and waterways, and each has its own characteristics. Four are described below.

Gardens

There are 16 million gardens in the UK and even more households have access to one. In Greater London, 3.8 million individual plots (front, side and back gardens) cover 24 per cent

of the area (37,900 hectares) and contain 2.5 million trees. Domestic gardens cover a similar proportion in other conurbations too. In one city that has been studied, Sheffield, there are an estimated 25,000 ponds, 45,000 nest boxes, 50,000 compost heaps and 360,000 trees taller than two metres in gardens.

Across the UK, gardens collectively make up a habitat larger than the Peak District, Cairngorms and Snowdonia National Parks put together (around 8,100 square kilometres), about ten per cent of available land area.

Allotments

The number of allotments reached its peak during the two World Wars, when there were about 1.4 million; in 2008, about 330,000 people held an allotment, ranging in size between 50 and 400 square metres. And allotments, as sites to grow food, are going to be attractive to a lot of mammals other than gardeners.

Cemeteries

Big, municipal cemeteries were built in the mid-nineteenth century, often on urban fringes, and were regarded as much as public landscapes, akin to parks, as they were burial places. There are between 12,000 and 20,000 cemeteries, churchyards and burial grounds in England and Wales today, including those that are no longer open. At least 6,000 of the latter are maintained for their wildlife and many cemeteries have been designated 'Sites of Special Scientific Interest'. In London, over 147 cemeteries have been identified as being of nature conservation importance, covering an area of almost 1,300 hectares.

A typical cemetery might be between two and four hectares (5–10 acres) of semi-natural grassland – either long meadow grasses with flowers such as ox-eye daisy, or shorter grass that supports species such as orchids. Bats lay perhaps the greatest claim to churches among mammal species but churchyards and cemeteries are often home to mice, voles, shrews and foxes too, and are large enough to support species as big as deer.

Brownfield sites

While all the talk is of green spaces, we should not forget brown ones. Sites that have had a permanent structure on them but are no longer in use are known as brownfield land. They can be eyesores and targets for anti-social behaviour but they can also be extraordinary places for biodiversity. Brownfield sites – such as derelict land and buildings, disused railway lines and airfields, quarries and brick-pits – have characteristics very different from those of other green spaces, providing specialist habitats that can support unique communities of species.

They can be particularly good for invertebrates: demolished buildings and piles of rubble are ideal habitats to nest and overwinter for many invertebrate species and patches of bare ground provide basking, burrowing and feeding sites for others.

Brownfield sites are often undisturbed and are sometimes contaminated, such that dominant weeds tend not to grow and instead a more diverse community of wild flowers develops.

There are about 64,000 hectares of brownfield land in England, about half of which is derelict or vacant. Forty per cent of brownfield sites, particularly those in London, are important for biodiversity according to *Buglife*, the invertebrate conservation charity, and a study in the West Midlands by Steven Falk found that the rarity of insects at the best brownfield sites was matched only by that in the best ancient woodlands. And where there are lots of invertebrates, larger beasts will follow. A study of two brownfield sites in Wales by Jan Miller found that many wild plants, invertebrates, amphibians, mammals and birds were more abundant there than anywhere in the surrounding countryside.

Safe havens

For some, such as foxes, urban sites can offer an alternative way of life; for others they can act as 'green corridors' or 'stepping stones', linking habitats that are too small to support communities alone; and for yet others, such as hedgehogs, they can be refugia as the rural landscape changes. For us they can be a remedy.

Urban mammals are only some of the mammals that occur more widely – but they are the ones that most of us are literally closest too. Most are overlooked – they're not as visible or as noisy as the birds in our towns and cities, which have an army of sympathetic supporters – but, when we take the time to look, it can be surprising who we find our neighbours to be.

About this book

Species accounts form the main part of this book, divided into the 'top ten' (commoner) species and those that are less ubiquitous residents of urban areas. Each account gives the common and scientific names (the latter always italicised and in two parts, the genus name first – with an initial capital – and the species name second) and a description of the species' appearance and behaviour.

Subheadings give details of:

Appearance Distinctive features that can be used to recognise the species.

Head–body length The length of a typical adult from the tip of the snout to the base of the tail.

Tail or ear length The length of the tail or ears compared with the body or head.

Weight The range of weight (in grammes or kilogrammes) of the adult population.

Lifespan The typical age that an adult lives to in the wild; sometimes a maximum recorded age either of a wild or a captive animal is given.

Reproduction The time of year that animals mate and give birth and the age that offspring are weaned.

Diet The main prey or type of food eaten.

Activity The time of year that the species is most active and whether it is active during the day (diurnal) or during the night (nocturnal).

Habitat The type of environment a species tends to live in.

Predators Species that feed on the animal.

Threats Factors that are or may affect the long-term survival of a population.

Status & conservation Whether a species is native or not, how common or scarce it is, whether it is of conservation concern, and some of the legislation that protects it.

Population size & distribution An estimate of how big the population is and how it is changing in the long term. Counting mammals – even large ones such as deer – is notoriously difficult and, for many species, estimates are 'best guesses' given limited data. Figures are the number of adults before offspring are born and are given for a particular region (e.g. Scotland or Great Britain); an estimate of the urban population is given separately when possible.

> Estimates of population size are based on those in a review by Stephen Harris, Pat Morris, Stephanie Wray and Derek Yalden (1995) and updated in *Mammals of the British Isles: Handbook, 4th Edition*, edited by S. Harris and D. W. Yalden (2008).

The distribution of the species in the British Isles is indicated on a map, showing where the species might be encountered. Areas with only rare or individual records are not shown.

Field signs: Many mammals are active mostly at dusk or during the night and are wary of people. Signs such as footprints, burrows or runs, droppings, or food remains are useful clues to the presence of an animal that might not have been seen.

A glossary at the end of the book explains many of the terms used and others that might be encountered in books about mammals.

Common urban species

The wild mammals in Britain belong to eight taxonomic groups, called 'orders' (see *A brief taxonomy*, page 92), and, of the six whose members are terrestrial, all but one have representatives recorded in the built environment. The odd one out – the red-necked wallaby – is a marsupial and far from home in quite a different sense as well.

Over twenty species are recorded in surveys of gardens and urban areas but some are more urbanite than others, turning up more frequently or at a greater number of sites. The most ubiquitous are probably wood mice. In one study of (more or less) randomly-selected households in Bristol, wood mice were found at four-fifths (17 of 21 gardens). In the same study, seven out of eight non-garden sites (allotments, cemeteries, scrub and woodland) were home to bank voles. In addition to these two species, grey squirrels, bats, foxes and hedgehogs are the most commonly-recorded mammals in surveys of urban sites by volunteers.

One of these is the People's Trust for Endangered Species' *Living with Mammals* survey, which has recorded grey squirrels, foxes and bats at around seven, six and five of every ten sites respectively. The caveat to this is that such sites are likely to be special cases – people are less likely to take part or return a survey form if there is nothing to report – but they show that urban sites are frequently home to several wild mammal species. In the case of *Living with Mammals*, two-thirds of sites are home to between three and seven mammal species.

Urban species are sometimes characterised as 'adapters' and 'exploiters'. Most urban mammals are of the first sort – only house mice and black rats are urban exploiters among the mammals in Britain. These are species that are so reliant on human activities that they are found only (or at least, very largely) in urban environments. Most, however, are urban adapters, taking advantage of both urban and rural environments, and some, like grey squirrels and foxes, do this with aplomb.

European badger *Meles meles*

Badgers, in contrast to many urban mammals, are more likely to be unwitting urban residents as built areas have grown up around established groups; but, regardless of their new neighbours, badgers can do well in urban areas. Cities such as London, Bristol, Bath and Birmingham have sizable numbers of badgers: a study in the 1980s found 80 groups living in the north-western part of Bristol.

Badgers have short, powerful legs and strong claws, making them very capable diggers. They excavate extensive burrows, called setts, made up of tunnels and chambers, sometimes at several levels, that are shared by up to two dozen adults, together with cubs. In Britain, badgers live in larger groups than those in continental Europe and display a greater range of social behaviours, centred around the setts in the group's home range. In urban areas, the boundaries of home ranges are less well defined and overlap more with those of other groups.

Setts can extend over hundreds of square metres and have many large entrances. The spoil heaps outside them, in contrast to those at fox earths, contain grass and other plant material, used as

KEY FEATURES

Appearance
Badgers are instantly recognisable: two dark stripes run the length of their white snout, perhaps acting as a signal to warn off predators. They are stocky with short, powerful legs and have especially large claws on their forefeet.

Head–body length	Tail length	Weight
65–80 cm (on average, males are larger than females).	12–17 cm	8–12 kg (occasionally up to 18 kg)

bedding. One study of setts in Birmingham and the Black Country found that they were typically in green suburban areas and often close to railways and canals.

Badgers emerge around dusk to forage and to groom themselves and other members of the group. Smell is the most important means of communication, identifying individuals and marking out group ranges.

Reproduction Mating peaks in spring but development of the young is delayed until winter and most litters are born in February. Usually only one female in a group will reproduce successfully, producing one to three cubs (and up to five on rare occasions). They leave the sett for the first time at about eight weeks but suckling may continue for four to five months. Unlike other social carnivores, cubs are not the centre of attention for other group members and have to take care to integrate themselves with resident adults.

Lifespan Typically seven to eight years but can be up to 16 years.

Diet In urban areas, badgers rely less on earthworms and more on a greater variety of foods than do rural badgers. Scavenged food, from rubbish bins, compost heaps, bird tables and that put out by people, made up a quarter of the diet over a year in one study; invertebrates (such as earthworms and cockchafer larvae), fruits, flower bulbs and vegetables also make up significant portions of the diet at different times of the year. Occasionally, small animals, such as hedgehogs and rodents, are also eaten.

Habitat Gardens, golf courses and embankments in urban areas and, more widely, a mix of deciduous woodland, open pasture and fields.

Predators Few natural predators in Britain but cubs are sometimes killed by dogs, foxes and other badgers.

Threats Road traffic accidents and illegal persecution. Disease (gut parasites) can be a major risk to cubs in their first year.

Status & conservation Native, common and widespread. Badgers and their setts are fully protected in the UK under The Protection of Badgers Act 1992.

Population size & distribution UK population about 300,000. The population has increased over the last ten years. Badgers are widely distributed throughout Britain and Ireland but are scarcer in Scotland. They are absent from most offshore islands except Anglesey, Arran, Canvey, Wight, Sheppey and Skye.

Activity Badgers are much less active during winter but do not properly hibernate and will forage outside the sett in mild weather. They are mostly crepuscular and nocturnal. A study of suburban badgers in Bristol found that they emerged later and foraged over a smaller area on nights with moonlight and clear skies.

FIELD SIGNS

Footprints usually show all five toes in front of a broad, kidney-shaped palm pad; long claw marks are visible.

Numerous small holes dug in lawns can be an indication of badgers foraging for earthworms and insect larvae.

Well-worn paths lead from setts, which can have large heaps of excavated soil outside. Spoil heaps contain discarded bedding (such as bracken, straw and leaves), which isn't found in the spoil from fox earths.

Bats

Seventeen species of bat breed in Britain and most will make use of buildings to roost in; pipistrelles and brown long-eared bats are the most urbanite species but serotines and Daubenton's might also be spotted in built-up areas.

Bats rarely cause any damage to buildings: unlike birds, they don't bring in nesting materials and, unlike rodents, they won't gnaw electric cables or wood. Their droppings carry no disease and are generally odourless. Large colonies of pipistrelles can number several hundred individuals in summer and can be noisy tenants, but so important are buildings to bats that managing and renovating them appropriately is a big part of bat conservation.

The construction industry is obliged to take into account the welfare of bats in the planning and building of all new developments but little is known about the suitability of building materials for bats.

Brown long-eared bat

Common and soprano pipistrelles

Soprano pipistrelles are slightly smaller than common pipistrelles and show a preference for lakes and rivers as foraging sites. In most aspects, the two species are difficult to tell apart – unless you have a bat detector. The echolocation calls of pipistrelles, like those of most bat species, are too high-pitched for people to hear without using a detector, which converts the sound to a lower pitch. The calls of soprano pipistrelles are slightly higher than those of common pipistrelles (around 55 kHz compared with 45 kHz).

Most bats look for warm roost sites in the summer, often on the south or west side of buildings. Pipistrelles are often found in tight spaces around the edges of roofs, beneath tiles, under roofing felt or in cracks. They readily make use of new buildings and there are many colonies in houses built since the 1960s. In winter, they hibernate in colder sites in buildings or trees.

Pipistrelles are amongst the smallest mammals in Britain, weighing about the same as a twenty-pence coin. From early summer to autumn, when they are active, pipistrelles emerge about 20 minutes after sunset, flying quickly five to ten metres above the ground in pursuit of small, flying insects. They catch their prey with their wings or tail membrane.

There is evidence that pipistrelles are less inhibited by light than are many other bat species and, like serotines, have been recorded feeding on insects attracted to street lights.

KEY FEATURES

Appearance
Dark-brown fur and a slightly paler underside. With their wings folded, they could fit into a standard matchbox.

Head–body length	Wing span	Weight
35–45 mm	19–23 cm	3–7 g

Reproduction Mating occurs in autumn and females gather to form maternity roosts the following spring. A single pup, or occasionally twins, is born between early June and mid-July.

Lifespan Typically two to three years; a few reach ten years or more.

Diet Midges, small flies, mosquitoes, lacewings and small moths are caught in the air.

Habitat Open woodland, farmland and suburban gardens; they often feed over water and along woodland edges and hedges. Soprano pipistrelles prefer to forage in habitats associated with water, such as lakes and riparian woodland, and may be more specialist feeders than common pipistrelles.

Predators Domestic cats.

Threats Susceptible to insecticides and chemicals used to treat roof timbers.

Status & conservation Native and common. All British bats and their roosts are protected by law.

Population size & distribution GB population 1,280,000 (common pipistrelles); 720,000 (soprano pipistrelles). Populations have declined by about 55 per cent since the 1960s but more recently (from 1998) common pipistrelles have increased and soprano pipistrelles have remained stable. Pipistrelles are widely distributed across the country but may be absent, or only rarely present, on some of the Scottish islands.

Activity Pipistrelles usually make a single foraging trip each night, emerging about 20 minutes after sunset. They hibernate between September and April but are sometimes active in winter if temperatures are mild.

FIELD SIGNS

Droppings are black and about 6–9 mm long, often on walls or under the exits of roosts.

Although echolocation calls are inaudible without a bat detector, pipistrelles in large colonies can be heard calling before emerging and during feeding. Calls warding off other individuals are also sometimes audible. Calls recorded with a frequency division or time expansion bat detector can be analysed with software (such as *Avisoft-SASLab Lite*, *Bat Scan* or *Wavesurfer*), which shows the calls as 'sonograms'. The echolation calls of a common pipistrelle are shown right, using *BatSound*. The frequency of the original calls was ten times that of the recordings (shown on the vertical axis). The time between calls (along the bottom) is less than a tenth of a second.

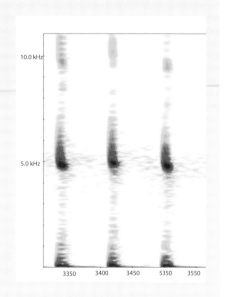

Brown long-eared bat *Plecotus auritus*

Brown long-eared bats emerge around an hour after sunset and often follow linear features such as hedges, streams or fences to and from feeding sites. Most bats use buildings seasonally, when maternity colonies are established during the summer, but brown long-eared bats will sometimes occupy the same building throughout the year.

They are found in villages and suburban areas (but rarely in urban environments), using the large, open roof spaces of older houses, churches and barns for summer roosts. Individuals or small groups are often found in crevices or around chimneys and ridge ends inside a loft. Hibernation sites include cellars and outbuildings, as well as mine tunnels and underground constructions.

Brown long-eared bats are bigger than pipistrelles, with broad wings that make them agile fliers. They fly comparatively low and slowly, close to vegetation, either catching flying insects or picking them off leaves or tree bark. Larger prey is sometimes taken to a perch and consumed while the bat hangs upside down, leaving piles of moth wings and other remains, on the ground below.

KEY FEATURES

Appearance
Brown long-eared bats (along with the much rarer grey long-eared) have unmistakable ears, about three-quarters the length of their body, that are held upright in flight. At rest, the ears are less noticeable, tucked under the wings or curled back like ram's horns. They have long, light-brown fur on their backs and creamy or white undersides, with pinkish faces.

Head–body length	Wing span	Weight
37–52 mm	23–28 cm	6–12 g

Reproduction Mating occurs between October and April but fertilisation and development are delayed until the following spring. Groups of 10-30 females form maternity roosts in late spring and, unlike other species, will share them with males. A single young is born in late June to mid July and is independent within six weeks.

Lifespan Typically four to five years in the wild; there are records of individuals in Britain re-caught after 13 years, and after 30 years on the Continent.

Diet Moths, beetles, flies, caddis flies, beetles and earwigs.

Habitat Typically woodland.

Predators Domestic cats, owls and kestrels.

Threats Habitat loss (and the loss of roost sites); and insecticides, which reduce the abundance of prey.

Status & conservation Native and common. All British bats and their roosts are protected by law.

Population size & distribution UK population 245,000 (they are the second most abundant bat in Britain). Surveys of hibernation roosts indicate a stable population in recent years. They are widely distributed throughout Britain and Ireland but absent from mountainous regions of northern Scotland and some Scottish islands.

Activity Hibernates from November to late March. They fly relatively frequently during the winter, particularly when the temperature rises above 4°C.

FIELD SIGNS

Droppings are brown or black, 8-10 mm long and often shiny because of the moth scales they contain. Food perches can sometimes be identified from piles of discarded remains and droppings. In flight, they have a distinctive silhouette, with long, extended ears.

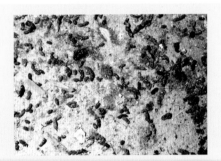

Other bats in the built environment

Daubenton's *(Myotis daubentonii)* and serotines *(Eptesicus serotinus)* also make use of the built environment. Daubenton's are sometimes seen circling over calm water such as ponds and lakes and hunt by skimming over the water surface and grabbing prey with their feet. Summer roosts are often in bridges and tunnels, and the network of canals that was built in Britain during the Industrial Revolution, along with the bridges that span them, provides ideal feeding and roost sites for the species.

Serotines are one of the largest bats in Britain, with wingspans over 30 cm. They often feed along roads and around street lights, and make extensive use of buildings for summer and hibernation roosts, especially older buildings and churches.

Bats and the importance of buildings

Kelly Gunnell,
Bat Conservation Trust

Loss of natural roosts has increased the importance of man-made structures for bats to the point that artificial roosts are becoming essential in the survival of many species. However, even these man-made roosts are now under threat: demolition of old buildings, renovations, changes in use, artificial lighting and the move towards air-tight buildings, all have implications for bat populations using buildings.

Brown long-eared bats nesting between rafters.

But creating and enhancing sites in developments can redress the balance. Spaces within new buildings tend to be inaccessible, removing the nooks and crannies generally used by bats. Designing in access points and roost spaces for bats (and birds, such as swifts) is a simple way to support more species in the built environment.

Bats that use buildings can generally be divided into four categories, depending on their requirements:

Crevice-dwelling bats (often hidden from view), e.g. pipistrelles, Brandt's bat and whiskered bat

Roof-void dwelling bats (sometimes visible on roof timbers), e.g. serotine and Leisler's bat

Bats that need flight space within roosts, e.g. Natterer's bat, and brown and grey long-eared bats

Bats that need flight space and flying access into roosts, e.g. greater and lesser horseshoe bats

Crevice-dwelling bats are the easiest to accommodate as they only require small gaps of 1.5–2 cm between surfaces to roost in. Bat boxes, especially those integrated into walls, such as the *Habitat* (shown below), are most suitable for this type of bat. If possible, create larger areas for bat roosts, such as lofts or bat houses, for species that require flying space.

Features to think about when providing roost sites:

Temperature Temperature is the key consideration in roost design. In contrast to people, bats look for warm roosts in the summer and cool sites in the winter. Generally, the optimum temperature for maternity roosts in the summer is 30–40°C. As a rule, locate roosts in the southern part of buildings but it is always best to provide a number of different sites for bats within a roost so that they can choose a suitable temperature based on their needs.

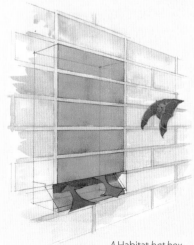
A Habitat bat box

Access Most bats enter roosts via small gaps 1.5–2 cm in width. Access can be provided by gaps in the exterior cladding, holes in soffits or by specially designed products such as bat access bricks, and should be 2–7 m above the ground. Locating roost entrances close to sizeable vegetation and flight lines, allows bats to emerge earlier and forage longer.

Materials Materials for roosts should be rough (for grip), non-toxic or corrosive, and with no risk of entanglement. They should also have suitable thermal properties that minimise daily fluctuations but allow summer roosts to warm up.

Gaps in cladding provide roost sites for pipistrelles.

Lighting Bats are nocturnal animals and are adapted to low-light conditions. This means that most species are disturbed by artificial lighting. Artificial lights shining on bat roosts, their access points or the flight paths away from the roost must always be avoided.

Surrounding landscape It is important to provide the correct planting and landscape features to attract bats in the first place. This is largely through maintaining or creating good foraging areas for bats by establishing areas that attract insects, especially nocturnal ones. Proximity to vegetation, linear features such as hedges and tree-lines, and access to water are all important.

The Bat Conservation Trust has a helpline giving advice and information (0845 1300 228) and other useful resources are given in *Further reading*, page 100.

Brown long-eared bats cluster in a roof space.

Brown rat *Rattus norvegicus*

Rats get a largely unfair press – portrayed as disreputable disease-carriers – but the wild cousins of the fancy rats kept as pets are intelligent, adaptable animals and, while they can carry some human diseases, the risk to most people is very small. As long as an area isn't overrun by them, they can be engaging neighbours.

Brown rats probably arrived in Britain in the 1700s, accidental stowaways aboard trade ships from Russia, but elsewhere they have lived alongside people for as long as there have been grain stores or food has been thrown away. Farm buildings can be home to colonies of typically several hundred individuals, made up of smaller social units or 'clans', but in domestic buildings, groups are a lot smaller. In 2007, the *English House Condition Survey* found that rats occupied four of every thousand urban properties and were present in the gardens of eight times as many (three per cent).

Rats have an intimate knowledge of their surroundings: they are suspicious of changes and might avoid unfamiliar objects for several days. Sniffing and grooming are important social behaviours. In small, well-fed groups, rats groom meticulously but as colonies become more crowded, they groom

KEY FEATURES

Appearance
Brown rats are larger than mice or voles, with grey-brown fur and a long, scaly tail, which is used to help balance. In water, they can be distinguished from water voles by their more pointed face, prominent ears and longer tail. Young rats have sleeker, greyer fur than that of adults.

Head–body length	Tail length	Weight
15–28 cm	A little shorter than the head-body length.	200–400 g

less and scuffles between individuals are more common. They have keen senses of hearing and smell and use scent and short, ultrasonic calls to communicate. They may also use ultrasound to echolocate in a similar way to bats.

Rats tend to follow familiar routes to get from one place to another and well-trodden paths (runs) can be spotted with practice. They are excellent swimmers (both on the surface and underwater) and can climb, readily getting into the upper storeys of buildings. They dig extensive burrows, often in sloping ground or the sides of ditches, or beneath flat stones or tree roots, and burrows may be used for several generations.

Reproduction Up to five litters are born in a year, each of 6–11 pups that are weaned by about three weeks. Young rats look similar to adult mice but have much broader hindfeet and relatively thicker tails.

Lifespan Very few live longer than a year in the wild.

Diet Urban rats feed on a wide range of foods but prefer starch- or protein-rich foods such as cereals. They will eat meat, fish, bones, fruit and invertebrates, and in agricultural areas feed on root crops.

Habitat Buildings such as houses and warehouses, where they can nest in floor cavities or beneath floorboards, and around farms, rubbish tips, sewers and urban waterways. Away from built areas, they live around cereal or root crops in hedgerows or ditches.

Predators Cats, foxes and owls kill young rats and, less commonly, adults.

Threats In particular circumstances or when numbers are high, they are killed as a pest.

Status & conservation Non-native and common.

Population size & distribution GB population (brown rat) 7,000,000; around 1,000,000 live in or close to urban premises. The population trend is unknown. Brown rats are widely distributed throughout the British Isles but are absent from most exposed mountain regions.

Activity Active throughout the year and mostly nocturnal but will take advantage of opportunities to feed during daylight.

FIELD SIGNS

Droppings are about 21 mm long and pointed at both ends, looking a little in size and appearance like olive stones.

Burrows are generally 6–9 cm in diameter and often on sloping ground or beneath cover such as flat stones or tree roots. Excavated earth is left by the entrance.

Footprints are sometimes visible in soft mud along water edges or in dusty environments such as grain stores, often with tail swipes. Runs in buildings are marked by dark smears on wood or brickwork; outside, they can appear as straight, shallow furrows in grass or well-worn trails of bare earth.

Almost all the rats in Britain today are brown rats. Its close relative, the **black rat, *Rattus rattus***, is one of our rarest mammals, with perhaps only a single permanent population of about 1,000 on the Shiant Isles in the Hebrides. Small numbers of black rats still occur around some ports, such as Southwark in London and Avonmouth in the Severn Estuary, bolstered by accidental migrants, but fail to establish permanent groups.

Black rats, however, can claim precedence. They arrived here on Roman ships and, until the last century, were widespread in towns and cities.

Compared with brown rats, black rats are smaller (half the weight) with longer, thinner tails and almost hairless ears, and tend to live almost exclusively inside buildings. They are more agile climbers than brown rats and show a preference for nesting high up in roof spaces, giving them their other name of 'roof rats'

The fortunes of black rats in Britain have been decided by brown rats, which are larger and hardier in a cold climate, but also by the modernisation of food stores and of the dockyards, with the advent of container ports, which had been their last stronghold.

Grey squirrel *Sciurus carolinensis*

The first grey squirrels in Britain were a pair brought from North America to Henbury Park in Cheshire in 1876. About 30 introductions followed at different sites in England and Wales (including Woburn Park in Bedfordshire, originally in 1889) and to three sites in Scotland, before their import was banned in 1937. By the start of the twentieth century, grey squirrels had made it to Regent's Park in London and were an addition to parks and private collections across the country.

Grey squirrels are agile climbers but spend a lot of time on the ground foraging. They nest in dens made in tree hollows or build large, spherical nests of woven twigs and leaves (called dreys) in the forks of tree trunks or branches. They swap between different nest sites every few days and it is common for two or more unrelated squirrels to share a nest. Urban grey squirrels will use other nest sites as well, including bird boxes, in roofing thatch and under tiles. They are frequent residents of church towers and have been known to nest in cavity walls.

Grey squirrels have home ranges of five to ten hectares in deciduous woodland but the size of those in urban and suburban areas has not been measured. They are solitary for most of the time, but

KEY FEATURES

Appearance
Predominantly grey, with a brown tinge along their backs; in summer, their flanks and legs can be a lot browner, and black and albino grey squirrels are common in some parts of England. Grey squirrels are larger than their red counterparts (weighing almost twice as much) and lack the winter ear tufts sported by red squirrels..

Head–body length	Tail length	Weight
24–28 cm	19–24 cm	400–600 g

establish a pecking order among individuals; when two squirrels meet, one indicates its dominance by bringing its ears forward (so that the white back of the ear is visible), foot stamping and flicking its tail. Eleven different vocal calls have been identified, including a repetitive barking to warn others of intruders.

Grey squirrels divide opinion: some people see them as a nuisance – stripping bark from trees, making a noise in roof spaces or pilfering bulbs – but to many others they have an undeniable appeal. They are adept problem-solvers and learn from watching their peers, particularly if it relates to stealing food. Their acrobatics on garden bird-feeders or bold advances in parks are an opportunity to watch a wild animal investigate its environment and more entertaining than a lot on TV.

Reproduction Two litters of two to four kits are born each year, one from February to April and another from July to November. The young are weaned between eight and ten weeks and are independent from three to six months.

Lifespan Most die in their first year; those that survive can live four to five years in the wild.

Diet Acorns, beech mast, flowers, nuts, bulbs, tree bark, fungi and tree shoots. They will also eat insects and occasionally birds' eggs.

Habitat Gardens, parks and areas with mature trees in urban areas, and primarily in broad-leaved and mixed woodland more widely.

Predators Stoats, foxes and domestic cats.

Threats Road traffic accidents, particularly in the autumn when juveniles are dispersing.

Status & conservation Non-native and common.

Population size & distribution GB population 2,600,000 (England, 2,000,000). The population is likely to be increasing. Grey squirrels are widely distributed throughout England and Wales and are edging their way into Scotland and Northern Ireland. They are absent from Europe except for a small but expanding area in Northern Italy.

Activity Active during the day, all through the year; in summer, they are usually most active two to four hours after sunrise and two to four hours before sunset. During bad winter weather, they may remain in their nest for one or two days.

FIELD SIGNS

Dreys are much more conspicuous than dens, which – unless you see a squirrel entering or leaving – are nearly impossible to identify. Dreys are about 30 cm in diameter and often built amongst climbing plants such as ivy or honeysuckle. From the ground, they can be mistaken for large birds' nests, but are usually in more sheltered sites than birds' nests, in clefts or close to the trunk (birds are more likely to nest in the crown of the tree) and tend to be high up (above 5 m).

Squirrels open hazelnuts by splitting the shell into two pieces, unlike mice and voles, which gnaw a round hole in the shell. 'Cores' of conifer cones with their scales stripped off are also characteristic of squirrels – birds leave cones with split scales. During late summer and autumn, food is hoarded in lots of small caches – several hazelnuts or beech masts buried just below the soil surface, for example – sometimes in the middle of a lawn or in borders, which have the bonus of 'caches' of spring bulbs supplied by gardeners.

Hazlenuts opened by squirrels are shown here between nuts opened by wood mice (on the left) and bank voles (on the right).

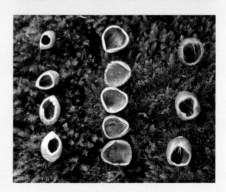

Red squirrel (*Sciurus vulgaris*) numbers declined drastically between 1900 and 1925, before grey squirrels had become established but, over the last century, greys have replaced reds over almost all of England and Wales, largely by 'out-competing' them.

Grey squirrels are no more aggressive to reds than they are to other greys but they have three competitive advantages: they are able to digest acorns, which red squirrels cannot, and so benefit from an extra food source; they live at greater densities in broad-leaved woodlands than reds do, reducing the amount of food such as hazelnuts available to red squirrels; and they are immune to squirrel pox virus, which is usually fatal to red squirrels.

Where red squirrels are still present – in large parts of Scotland and Ireland, and in North Cumbria and Northumberland, and islands such as Anglesey, Jersey and the Isle of Wight – they can be as urbanite as greys and take full advantage of gardens. Like greys, red squirrels can breed twice a year but are much less likely to reproduce if food is scarce. Putting food (such as sunflower seeds, hazelnuts, cob nuts, carrot and apple) out every few days, can be a valuable extra to their diet, particularly in the summer before fruits and nuts are ripe, and can support a breeding population.

Hedgehog *Erinaceus europaeus*

Hedgehogs are a familiar urban mammal. They can be regular garden visitors and their distinctive spiny appearance means they are unlikely to be mistaken for anything else. Hedgehogs feed on soil invertebrates, such as earthworms and beetles, and the mown grass of garden lawns and recreational ground can be an ideal foraging habitat. Their consumption of caterpillars, which make up about a quarter of their prey, and slugs, is appreciated by gardeners as pest control. Hedgehogs are active mostly during the night and can be heard snuffling through undergrowth or snorting during courtship and fights. During the day they sleep in long grass (making them vulnerable to garden strimmers), concealed in loosely constructed nests.

About 5,000 closely-packed hollow, creamy-white spines, each about two to three centimetres in length and tapering to a sharp point, cover the back and flanks of an adult. At their base, the spines are brown, but their tips are pure white with a dark, chocolate-brown band just behind the point. The hedgehog's loose skin allows it to roll up into a tight ball, drawing in its head, tail and legs so that they are completely hidden, and by pulling the spines upright so that they point outwards hedgehogs can protect themselves against most natural enemies.

Urban hedgehogs prefer the invertebrate-rich gardens of semi-detached and terraced houses over those of detached houses and roadside verges, occupying home ranges of 10–30 hectares.

KEY FEATURES

Appearance
Hedgehogs have a short inconspicuous tail, small ears and surprisingly long legs, usually hidden under a 'skirt' of long hairs. On their underside, they have coarse grey-brown fur.

Head–body length	Tail length	Weight
Up to 30 cm	2 cm	450–1500 g

Home ranges overlap with each other and although they are not defended as exclusive territories, hedgehogs often have scuffles with other individuals they meet. Encounters between males sometimes involve head-butting. In a typical night, males might travel between one and three kilometres in open areas but move smaller distances in built-up areas.

Although they might be seen trundling most of the time, hedgehogs can run quickly when they want to, covering up to 40 metres in a minute, and sprinting at two metres per second over short distances. For the most part, they rely on their sense of smell to find food and to alert them to danger, unearthing prey with strong forelegs, adapted for digging.

Courtship involves the approach of a male towards a female who turns to keep her flank facing him. The pair circle around each other, sometimes for hours, making regular puffing and snorting noises (mainly those of the female). This often attracts other males, which are chased away. To mate, the female presses her belly to the ground and arches her back downwards, keeping her spines flat. After mating, males play no further role in rearing offspring and will court and mate with several females in a year.

Between November and the end of March, when food is scarce, hedgehogs hibernate to conserve energy, remaining largely inactive. Their heart rate decreases from 190 to 20 beats per minute and their body temperature falls to just a few degrees Celsius. The exact timing of hibernation depends on the age and sex of the hedgehog as well as the outside temperature.

Reproduction Up to seven offspring are born from May onwards, after a gestation of about four and a half weeks. Hoglets are born blind and without spines, which emerge soon after birth. The first set of white spines is replaced by darker ones that grow through. At about two weeks old, their eyes open and the young are weaned by about four weeks.

Lifespan About a half die before their first year; the average lifespan in the wild is about two years. A small percentage of individuals will reach five years of age.

Diet Mainly beetles, caterpillars and earthworms but also birds' eggs, other invertebrates, ripe fruits and carrion.

Habitat Urban sites such as gardens, golf courses and parks. Regent's Park in London is the only one of the Royal Parks where hedgehogs are still present. Rural habitats include woodland edges, hedgerows in meadowland and rough pasture. They avoid wet areas or large pine forests.

Predators Occasionally badgers and foxes.

Threats Habitat loss due to more intense agriculture and tidier, smaller gardens. The sort of slug pellets sold for use in gardens probably do not have an effect toxically but can reduce the abundance of prey. Road deaths may be important locally.

Status & conservation Hedgehogs are native and locally common. In 2007, hedgehogs were made a priority species in the UK Biodiversity Action Plan.

Population size & distribution GB population in 1995 was estimated to be 1,500,000 but it is likely to have declined since then. A recent report, *The State of Britain's Hedgehogs*, (www.ptes.org/publications) found that five separate surveys between 1996 and 2010 showed declines in both urban and rural areas. A conservative estimate is that a quarter of the population (nationally) has been lost in the last ten years (see *Further reading*, page 100). Hedgehogs are found throughout the British Isles but are absent from some of the Scottish Islands

Activity Bulky winter nests (hibernacula) are built in October and hedgehogs hibernate from about November through to March/April, remaining largely inactive. Occasionally, they will move between nest sites during the winter. During the rest of the year, they are active mostly at night or after heavy rainfall. Urban hedgehogs tend to be more active after midnight when the risk of encountering people or road traffic is less.

FIELD SIGNS

Trails can sometimes be seen winding through dewy grass in the morning but footprints are rarely visible. These tracks were recorded in a tunnel designed to monitor hedgehogs.

Hedgehog droppings are almost black, about the size of a little finger, and recognisable by the fragments of beetle prey that catch the light.

Mice

Two species of mouse are common in urban environments: wood mice and house mice, and, while their diminutive size and behaviour might seem unspectacular, their success in adapting to different habitats is extraordinary. After our own species, house mice are probably the most widespread mammal in the world, living independently of people as well as alongside them. House and wood mice have moved in with us and in many instances, have hitched a lift on our 'coat tails' – accidentally carried in trade and our belongings – and, as human populations have spread, so have those of the humble mouse.

Wood mouse

House mouse *Mus domesticus*

House mice arrived in Britain with Iron Age traders. They are predominantly an indoor mouse, occupying wall cavities, under-floor- and roof-spaces, and are rarely found in arable fields or hedgerows; of 1,536 small mammals caught on farmland in Wiltshire and Gloucestershire only five were house mice. Unlike wood mice, house mice do not occur in woodland, but are at home in the London Underground system, where they thrive in the warmth and on the litter thrown away by commuters.

In soft earth, house mice are efficient tunnellers and can dig complex burrows with several chambers and entrances, but in buildings they will use existing spaces, gnawing through wood and soft plastic to gain access. They can pass through gaps as narrow as one centimetre.

Individuals have been recorded travelling more than a kilometre in a single night but more usually will stay close to a single food source such as a grain store. They are agile climbers, making use of all three dimensions of their habitat, and are territorial, such that only a few dominant males will breed when conditions are crowded.

KEY FEATURES

Appearance
Grey–brown in colour, with large pink ears and a long, hairless tail. They have smaller eyes and hindfeet than wood mice and have a narrower head.

Head–body length	Tail length	Weight
6–10 cm	As long as the head and body.	12–22 g

Reproduction Five to ten litters of four to eight pups are born in a year. The young are weaned by two weeks and become sexually mature by five to six weeks. In her lifetime, a female may produce about 40 offspring.

Lifespan Up to 18 months in the wild but few survive longer than six months.

Diet Mainly grain and fruit, but also insects and other invertebrates, and almost anything edible.

Habitat House mice occur most commonly in buildings (including farm buildings such as poultry and pig units). In urban areas, they are found in flats, houses, shops, restaurants, warehouses and factories. In a few places, where there is no competition from wood mice (such as Stokholm and some other islands), they live independently of people.

Predators Barn owls, stoats, weasels, rats and domestic cats.

Threats Severe cold. Where they can damage and contaminate stored food products, they are killed, usually with poison.

Status & conservation Non-native and locally abundant.

Population size & distribution GB population 5,400,000. The population has been stable over the last 25 years. House mice are widely distributed throughout Britain and Ireland, including most inhabited small islands.

Activity Mainly nocturnal with periodic bouts of activity lasting several hours.

FIELD SIGNS

House mice leave several clues to their presence, including droppings, runways and gnawed food remains.

Droppings are about 7 mm long and accumulate in small mounds at particular sites.

Regular routes (runs) are marked by droppings and black smears.

Wood (or long-tailed field) mouse *Apodemus sylvaticus*

Wood mice are characteristic of woodland, living in the leaf litter, but they are found in habitats as diverse as farmland, sand dunes, hedgerows and road verges, and are common in green urban spaces such as gardens. They are very adaptable and opportunistic, readily taking advantage of food on bird tables and coming into houses during cold weather.

For a species as numerous and widespread as wood mice, you might imagine there is little new to discover about them – but think again. In 2003, it was found that wood mice make signposts to help them find their way back to places – the only species known to do so apart from our own. Piles of leaves, twigs or shells (that had been thought to hide nest-holes) are moved about by wood mice as they explore an area and used to relocate a site if they have to flee because of a predator or other disturbance.

A nest of leaves or shredded grass and moss is usually built underground; tunnels connect subterranean food stores, and burrows may survive from one generation to the next. Nests are also found within walls and in buildings.

KEY FEATURES

Appearance
Wood mice are recognisable by their large ears and black, bulging eyes. They are dark brown with a pale-grey underside and a small patch of yellowish fur between their front legs. Their tails are long and dark, with only sparse hair. In some areas, wood mice might be confused with yellow-necked mice *(Apodemus flavicollis)* (page 74), which are found in south and south-east England and central Wales, but wood mice are smaller and less orange in colour.

Head–body length	Tail length	Weight
8–11 cm	As long as the head and body.	16–18 g in winter; 25–27 g in summer.

Reproduction Litters of four to eight young are born between March and November, and females can have up to six litters in a year. The young are weaned by three weeks and are sexually mature within two months.

Lifespan Up to 20 months.

Diet Mainly seeds (such as acorn and sycamore), but also buds (especially blackberry), fruits, nuts, snails, insects, fungi, moss and tree bark.

Habitat They are found in most habitats and in urban areas, often present in gardens and buildings.

Predators Owls, foxes, mustelids, kestrels and domestic cats. In urban areas, they can make up between a quarter and a half of the prey of cats, probably limiting the population.

Threats Agricultural pesticides.

Status & conservation Native, widespread and common.

Population size & distribution GB population 38,000,000. The population trend is unknown. Wood mice are present throughout Great Britain and Ireland, including on most of the large islands and many of the small ones.

Activity Mainly nocturnal but occasionally active above ground during the day in summer.

FIELD SIGNS

Both wood mice and bank voles open hazelnut shells by gnawing a round hole, leaving tooth marks that look like the milled edge of a coin around the rim. Only wood mice, though, leave tooth marks on the outside of the shell as well.

Food is cached in burrows and places such as the corners of outhouses and garages.

A coarse dust of 'kibblings' is left behind after eating grain.

Nests are typically made of leaves in burrows or between tree roots, but can be under cover in buildings or (as opposite) in woodpiles.

Wood mice lack the musky smell characteristic of house mice.

Mole *Talpa europaea*

Moles belong to the same family as hedgehogs and shrews but have evolved a subterranean lifestyle. They dig extensive burrow systems, running from just below the surface to well over a metre down and covering several thousand square metres (0.2–0.4 hectares), and spend almost their entire lives underground. Their strong, broad forefeet are used one at a time to dig, while their hindfeet are braced against the walls of the tunnel.

The tunnel system acts as a pit-fall trap, collecting earthworms and insect larvae, which are caught by the patrolling resident before they can escape. In the darkness of the tunnels, moles locate prey with their fleshy snout, which is exquisitely sensitive to touch. Smell too seems to be important in finding food at short distances, and sensory hairs on their face, forelimbs and tail also detect their surroundings.

Moles are adapted to the low oxygen levels in tunnels (sometimes only a third of those at the surface) by having more blood and twice as much haemoglobin, the oxygen-carrying pigment in blood, than other mammals of their size.

Counting molehills is not a good indication of the number of moles in an area. When prey is plentiful, moles may be inconspicuous because the existing tunnels provide sufficient food and there is little

KEY FEATURES

Appearance
They have strong, shovel-like forelimbs and short, usually black fur that can lie in either direction, allowing them to move easily forwards and backwards through tunnels. Very small eyes are hidden in the fur.

Head–body length	Tail length	Weight
12–17 cm	2–4 cm	70–130 g

need to excavate new ones; when it is scarce, or in cold weather when earthworms descend to more temperate depths, the network of tunnels is extended in search of food, turning up fresh molehills. However, at least one study has shown the opposite effect: reducing earthworm numbers (by encouraging an acidic soil or by mowing or grazing) gives rise to fewer molehills.

Reproduction Moles breed from late February to June. Litters of three or four pups are born in April or May and are weaned at four to five weeks of age. They disperse shortly afterwards and are able to breed the following spring.

Lifespan Two-thirds die in their first year; adults typically survive two to three years. One per cent may reach six years.

Diet Mainly soil invertebrates such as earthworms, insect larvae, myriapods (centipedes and millipedes) and slugs. They will also feed on carrion.

Habitat Present in most habitats where the soil is sufficiently deep to dig tunnels. They thrive in pastures and arable fields, in addition to gardens.

Predators Tawny owls and stoats.

Threats Moles are considered a pest on agricultural land and are controlled by trapping. Poisoning with strychnine was banned in the UK in 2006.

Status & conservation Native, common and widespread.

Population size & distribution GB population 31,000,000. The population trend is unclear. There is an indication that numbers have declined since 2000. Moles are widespread on mainland Britain and the islands of Skye, Mull, Anglesey, Wight, Alderney and Jersey. They are absent from Ireland.

Activity At most times of the year, males and females forage for three 3-4 hour periods in each 24 hours, returning to their nest after each to rest for a similar length of time. In some instances, the activity patterns of neighbouring moles are synchronised. Moles are active throughout the year but molehills are most abundant in spring and autumn.

FIELD SIGNS

While moles themselves are rarely seen, molehills – conical spoils of earth pushed up from permanent tunnels – are easily spotted. In gardens, lawns tend to show the brunt of moles' handiwork; but rather than trying to remove moles from an area using kill-traps that are rarely humane, molehills can be put to good use (see *Possible conflicts*, page 82).

In some circumstances, particularly in low-lying areas prone to flooding or when the soil is shallow, larger structures (up to a metre high), called 'fortresses', are built. These usually contain a nest chamber above the ground level, which would otherwise be in deeper tunnels, and several radiating runs. They are built throughout the year, but mainly in winter, by both males and females, although not all moles build them.

Exploratory surface tunnels in soft or freshly cultivated earth push up ridges in the soil or appear as open trenches when their roofs collapse. These are particularly evident in spring and at one time were called 'traces d'amour', although it's unlikely that they are particularly to do with ardent males.

Stories of an "explosion in mole numbers" perennially pop up in the press: each year the story has it that the ban of the strychnine in 2006, which had been used to kill moles, has led to the population soaring as testified to by the increase in the call-out of registered mole catchers. The problem with such reports is that there is no real evidence behind them. The number of sites recording molehills in the PTES *Living with Mammals* survey has remained more or less constant since the survey began in 2003 (see page 89) and no surveys of the wider countryside have been carried out since the ban. The increase in call-outs is because the 3,000 or so farmers and landowners that had been licenced to use strychnine have had to turn to alternative methods. Moles are frequently demonised but it is a moot point whether their reputation as pests is deserved, or whether the measures used to control them are justified. The control of a native wild mammal should be informed by sound science and not unsupported claims. In gardens, moles push up some earth at times; but we shouldn't make a mountain out of a molehill.

Rabbit *Oryctolagus cuniculus*

Rabbits were present in Britain by the middle of the twelfth century CE, brought across by the Normans, as a source of meat and fur. Numbers increased in the wild after 1750 due to changes in agriculture and the growth of game-keeping, which kept down the numbers of predators such as polecats and buzzards. Today, they are a common sight in the countryside and in urban fringes, venturing into gardens and allotments, along road verges and railway embankments.

Rabbits dig burrows (warrens), which offer protection, and several social groups, typically of two to eight adults, share the network of tunnels. Males and, less so, females, establish separate pecking-orders within a group: dominant males father the majority of offspring in their group, while dominant females obtain the best nest sites. The dense, soft fur of rabbits loses heat quickly when it is wet, so rabbits keep dry, staying beneath ground during wet weather. They rarely venture further than 200 metres from the safety of the warren.

Rabbits rely on their keen hearing (enhanced by large, mobile ears) and speed to avoid predators. They are an important prey species for many carnivores and raptors, but they have a significant impact too as grazers. Rabbit numbers have fluctuated enormously in the last 100 years; in the early twentieth century there were around 100 million in England, Wales and Scotland, but between 1953

KEY FEATURES

Appearance
Their fur ranges from a light sandy colour to black, but is typically greyish-brown and paler on the animal's underside. They have long ears (that lack the black tips of those of hares) and long hindfeet.

Head–body length	Ear length	Weight
30–40 cm	About the same length as the head.	1.2–2.0 kg

and 1955, the viral disease myxomatosis killed over 99 per cent of the wild population. Without rabbits grazing, woody species became established and large areas of chalk downland reverted to scrub, changing the habitat and species that depended on it. Only when they were gone, was the importance of rabbits in our countryside – maintaining particular habitats and communities of species – appreciated fully.

The large blue butterfly, *Phengaris arion*, is one of those whose fortunes are ecologically tied to those of rabbits. It was declared extinct in Britain in 1979 but was reintroduced in the 1980s. After its second moult, the caterpillar of the large blue is taken underground by the red ant *Myrmica sabuleti*, which 'milks' it for secretions of its honey gland, while the caterpillar eats the ants' brood. Ten months later, it pupates and leaves the ant nest as a butterfly. The ants prefer areas of short sward where the soil is warmed and without rabbits to crop the grass, their numbers diminished and the decline of the large blue was hastened.

The collective weight of rabbits in Great Britain is more than that of any other terrestrial wild mammal (perhaps twice as much as red deer) and their impact can be a problem for forestry and agriculture as well as, on occasion, for gardeners (see *Possible conflicts*, page 85).

Reproduction Rabbits give birth to litters of three to seven offspring (called kits or kittens) in a 'nest stop', a blind-ended tunnel culminating in an enlarged chamber, which the female lines with grass and moss, and fur plucked from her belly. If food is plentiful, females can have litters every five to six weeks from February to August. The kittens are born blind, deaf and almost hairless; they can open their eyes after ten days and are weaned at about 25 days. They can breed from the age of four months.

Lifespan Only about one in ten newborn rabbits will survive their first year in the wild and few survive over two years old. In captivity rabbits can live to ten years.

Diet Grasses, cereal crops, root vegetables and young shoots of meadow plants. In winter they eat the bark of small trees.

Habitat The most suitable habitats are areas of short vegetation close to woodland or banks suitable for burrows. Lighter soils and well-drained grassland support the greatest numbers of rabbits. They are often found in gardens, parks and on recreational ground, such as golf courses, in built-up areas.

Predators Foxes, mustelids (such as stoats, weasels and badgers) and buzzards.

Threats Disease (Rabbit Haemorrhagic Disease and Myxoma virus).

Status & conservation Non-native, common; in Europe as a whole, the 2008 IUCN Red List classifies them as Near Threatened.

Population size & distribution UK population 38,000,000. The population has increased over the last 25 years but has fallen significantly over the last decade, especially in Scotland. Rabbits are widespread throughout Britain and Ireland below a height of 350 metres, but are absent from the Isle of Rum and the Isles of Scilly.

Activity Crepuscular and nocturnal but are also active during the day if they are not disturbed .

FIELD SIGNS

Burrows (often on slopes or banks) have entrances 10-50 cm in diameter and annual weeds and nettles, encouraged by the loose soil and high nitrogen levels, are often found around them. Entrances are sometimes marked by a heap of excavated soil.

Footprints in snow show the long prints of the hind feet and the smaller, round prints of the fore feet.

Red fox *Vulpes vulpes*

Foxes exploit the built environment with panache. They are intelligent, adaptable mammals, opportunistic, with unfussy palates, and have readily adapted to towns and cities, where they are more accustomed to people. In fact, more is known about urban foxes than about their rural counterparts.

Foxes began to colonise suburban areas of London in the 1930s, catching the public's attention in the 1960s. Today, there are about five thousand adult foxes within the M25 and perhaps seven times as many in urban areas nationally. Inner-city foxes tend to eat less caught prey than those in the suburbs, feeding more on scavenged food. The rich pickings that are available mean that urban foxes have smaller home ranges – typically about a tenth (10-100 ha) of those in rural areas – and foxes have been known to commute, foraging in urban areas at night while spending the day out of town.

They are social animals, living in family groups of a breeding pair, together with cubs in the spring,

KEY FEATURES

Appearance
In the summer, foxes lose the distinctive yellow-brown fur of their winter coat, appearing darker and scruffier while new, shorter fur grows through. Sometimes their bushy tail can be reduced to an almost furless vestige. The backs of their ears and front of their fore- and hindfeet are jet black.

Head–body length	Tail length	Weight
56–75 cm	Slightly more than half the head–body length.	4.0–9.5 kg The average weight (6.5 kg for males and 5.5 kg for females) is only a little heavier than that of a domestic cat.

and sometimes other subordinate juveniles and adults. The latter are usually young born the previous year and help with the rearing of cubs, feeding, grooming and playing with them. Each group occupies a territory, which is marked with urine and droppings (scats). Many dens are inside vacant or occupied buildings, often under floorboards, or under garden sheds. If necessary, foxes will dig extensive earths, particularly in well-drained soils, choosing sites in overgrown gardens – in flowerbeds, rockeries or under tree roots – or cemeteries, under grave stones. Elsewhere, they will make use of (disused or occupied) badger setts or old rabbit burrows.

Foxes hunt and scavenge with keen senses of smell and hearing, and probably use the latter to locate earthworms, which can make up a large part of their diet, as well as prey hidden in vegetation or snow. In 2011, it was found that foxes pounce most often – and most successfully – in a north-east direction, particularly when the prey is concealed. It is thought that they use the

Earth's magnetic field as a 'rangefinder', matching the angle of the sound to that of the magnetic field, which identifies a fixed distance in front of them.

Foxes communicate with each other using a wide range of calls, facial expressions and body postures, as well as scent markings. Twelve adult and eight pup vocalisations have been identified and 28 groups of sounds described.

Reproduction Foxes mate between December and February, and litters of four or five blind and deaf cubs are born between March and May. Mothers spend almost all of their time with the cubs for the first two to three weeks, receiving food from the male or other members of the group. The young are weaned at four weeks and are independent by the autumn, typically moving away between October and January.

Lifespan Few wild foxes live longer than two or three years; in two studies of urban foxes, the average life expectancy was 14 and 18 months. In captivity, they can live up to 14 years.

Diet Almost anything from field voles, garden birds (such as thrushes, sparrows and wood pigeons), earthworms and insects, to fruit and vegetables. In urban areas, they scavenge food from rubbish bins and gardens, and raid bird tables. Food put out by householders can make up about half of their diet. They will also scavenge road casualty carcasses and often stash food (in caches) to be consumed later.

Habitat Foxes use a range of urban habitats but prefer residential suburbs, favouring back gardens, allotments and rough ground. They have few specific habitat requirements and are most abundant in habitats that offer a wide variety of shelter and food. In rural areas, they live in woodland, scrub and farmland.

Predators Few natural predators but cubs may be killed by badgers and dogs. Most deaths are caused by humans.

Threats Road traffic, accidental and deliberate poisoning, and shooting.

Status & conservation Native, common and widespread. Hunting with dogs is illegal in England and Wales under the Hunting Act 2004 and is also illegal in Scotland.

Population size & distribution GB population 225,000 (rural); 33,000 (urban). There has been little change in the population over the last 10 years. Foxes are widely distributed in Britain and Ireland but are absent from all the Scottish islands, except Skye and Harris, and from the Scilly and Channel isles.

Activity Foxes can be active throughout the year and at any time during the day or night, but are particularly active at dusk and dawn. During the day, they are often seen sunning themselves on roofs.

FIELD SIGNS

Fox tracks are similar to those of a cat or small dog but are more diamond-shaped and longer than they are wide. The triangular rear (palm) pad is a similar size to the toe pads and a cross can be drawn between the pads without crossing any of them. Claw marks are usually visible (in contrast to those of cats, which retract their claws when walking or running). When walking or trotting, fox prints are 30-60 cm apart in a nearly straight line.

Barks and the loud contact calls made by both sexes, particularly in the winter, include a blood-curdling 'scream'.

Scats are left in conspicuous spots, such as on rockeries, around ponds and on patios, and fox urine has a distinctive musky odour.

Scattered feathers can indicate the site of a kill – carcasses are usually carried away and cached, and disturbed earth on lawns and flowerbeds can indicate the site of such hoards.

Voles

Three species of vole – bank, field and water voles – are widespread in Britain, while two subspecies of common vole are separately found on the islands of Guernsey and Orkney.

Bank and field voles are the most likely of the three to be found in urban areas but water voles have been spotted on rivers and canals in more than thirty towns and cities. (Urban conurbations may even be a stronghold for water voles: a survey in Birmingham and the Black Country in 1997 found that the decline in urban areas was not as dramatic as that at more rural sites.)

Although similar to wood mice, voles rely more on thick ground cover, which means they are not as urbanite as their murine relatives but, even so, voles are frequently caught by domestic cats and, bank voles particularly, are found in overgrown gardens and along road verges.

Bank vole

Bank vole *Myodes glareolus*

Bank and field voles are similar in size and appearance, but only bank voles are ever a deep chestnut colour. They make their nests in shallow burrows several centimetres below the surface, which they line with leaves, grasses, moss or feathers. Although they predominantly move around on the ground, they are agile climbers and use arboreal runways to reach haws and other fruit in hedges and bushes.

Home ranges vary in size between about 250 and 2,000 square metres depending on factors such as the season and type of habitat, and individuals typically stray less than 50 metres from the centre of the range. Bank voles are more active during the day than wood mice but are easily disturbed and will retreat with lightning speed to their burrow.

A distinct race (subspecies) of bank vole occurs on Skomer Island, off the south west coast of Wales, where it was probably introduced. It is paler in colour and slightly larger than its mainland relative, having an average body length of 10.5 centimetres compared with nine centimetres.

KEY FEATURES

Appearance
Bank voles have a reddish-chestnut coat with a dirty-white underside. They have small eyes and ears, and a blunt nose. At first sight, they might be confused with wood mice, but the latter have a longer tail and bound rather than scurry.

Head–body length	Tail length	Weight
8–12 cm	Less than half the body length.	14–40 g

Reproduction Litters of three to five blind, hairless young are born between April and October and become independent within nine weeks.

Lifespan Up to 20 months in the wild; very few survive two winters. Over half of those born early in the season will die before they are four months old.

Diet Green leaves make up to half of their diet; fruits and seeds, and small amounts of fungi, roots, flowers and invertebrates are also eaten.

Habitat They are common in deciduous woodland but also found in hedgerows, road verges, parks and gardens, where there is plenty of ground cover and food.

Predators Tawny owls, weasels and foxes.

Threats Habitat loss and agricultural pesticide use.

Status & conservation Native to Great Britain; populations in Ireland were possibly introduced in the 1920s from Germany. Common and widespread.

Population size & distribution GB population 23,000,000. The population trend is unknown. Bank voles are widely distributed throughout Britain and the south-west of Ireland.

Activity Bank voles are active during both the day and night, particularly at dawn and dusk during the summer.

FIELD SIGNS

Beechmast is scatter-hoarded in small caches of up to ten nuts just beneath the leaf litter or in tunnel walls. Like wood mice, bank voles open hazel nuts with a round hole that has visible tooth-marks around its edge, but unlike wood mice, the surface of the shell is unscratched.

Bank vole nests are usually below ground, but breeding nests can be in tree trunks. The burrow entrances of water voles (shown above) appear as a series of holes along the water's edge.

Water vole *(Arvicola amphibious)* numbers started to decline in Britain in the 1930s as changes in land use and the management of waterways reduced the amount of suitable habitat. The decline hastened in the 1980s because of predation by American mink and in 1998, the population was only a tenth of that in 1990.

Although mink make use of urban habitats (in 2009, the *Lincolnshire Echo* reported that mink had set up home next to their wharf offices in the centre of Lincoln), they are still scarce there, giving water vole populations some respite.

But urban areas are not entirely plain sailing for water voles. The urbanisation of waterways can lead to the fragmentation of populations, leaving small, isolated groups that are more likely to die out, and at sites where water voles co-exist with brown rats, which similarly make use of waterways and ponds, poison put down to get rid of the latter can have the same effect on water voles.

Weasel

Less commonly-encountered species

Alongside those species that are more or less ubiquitous in the built environment are those that are less commonly seen – either because they are scarce generally or because they do not make use of urban habitats as readily. Those that are scarce might be more familiar neighbours if they were more widespread. Red squirrels and fat dormice *(Glis glis)* have limited distributions in Britain but can be no less urbanite than more familiar species where they do occur. In mainland Europe, red squirrels commonly use gardens and are no more timorous than grey squirrels in Britain, and fat dormice are frequently recorded in gardens and roof-spaces of urban fringes on the Continent.

For some species, urban habitats might be less attractive: stoats and weasels, for example, find more abundant prey (rabbits and small rodents) in rural landscapes than around towns; for others, behavioural characteristics might be the reason for their absence. Pine martens and hazel dormice *(Muscardinus avellanarius)* are scarce in Britain but, where they do occur, they are much less urbanite than their taxonomic cousins beech martens *(Martes foina)* and garden dormice *(Eliomys quercinus)*, which are absent in Britain but widespread in mainland Europe. On the Continent, beech martens are established town-dwellers, with a reputation for getting in beneath the bonnets of cars during patrols of their territory, and garden dormice are commonly found in gardens and houses. The characteristic that they share is that they are less arboreal than their British counterparts, moving about more on the ground, and this might explain (at least in part) their more urban ways.

Deer

Roe deer and muntjac are established denizens of urban areas, but they are comparative newcomers. Muntjacs were brought to Britain in 1838 by John Russell Reeves and were kept at London Zoo in the first half of the nineteenth century. In 1894, six individuals were brought to Woburn Park in Bedfordshire and, in 1901, eleven were released into neighbouring woods. Further releases (and escapes) followed at other sites and the population spread.

Roe deer too, although considered native, were reintroduced into England in the nineteenth century from mainland European stock, after overhunting and the loss of woodland all but wiped them out. Today, muntjac and roe deer are found in urban parks, cemeteries and school grounds, as well as in allotments and gardens.

Roe deer

Reeves' (or Chinese) muntjac *Muntiacus reevesi*

Muntjacs are Britain's smallest deer but they can also be loud. They can be heard 'barking' for long periods, usually if they have been disturbed or when females are in 'heat' (oestrous). They can be difficult to spot in dense cover, particularly in summer when vegetation is at its thickest, but the more open spaces of gardens and allotments are excellent places to get a better view.

Between April and November, muntjacs are a reddish-brown colour with a lighter, often white, throat and underside. When alarmed, they run off with their broad tail held erect, so that its white underside is displayed.

KEY FEATURES

Appearance
Muntjacs are easily recognised by distinctive facial markings and posture. Black stripes run in a V-shape in males (from the base of each antler) and a kite shape in females, at the top of a ginger face. Prominent scent glands are present at the corner of each eye. Both sexes have large canine teeth (tusks) but only in males are they visible below the upper lip. Males have short, backward-pointing antlers that are used (along with their tusks) to spar with other males. Their haunches are higher than their withers (shoulders), which gives them a hunched-forward appearance.

Male

Female

Shoulder height	Weight
45–52 cm	12–15 kg

Reproduction Mating occurs at any time of year and females give birth to a single spotted fawn after seven months. Fawns survive even harsh winter conditions well.

Lifespan In the wild, about a fifth survive for five or more years; some may reach 10-12 years.

Diet Shoots and leaves of deciduous trees and garden plants, berries, acorns, chestnuts, seeds, bark and to a lesser extent grasses.

Habitat In suburban areas, large gardens and areas of shrub; they prefer habitats with lots of different vegetation providing dense cover.

Predators Occasionally foxes and dogs.

Threats Road traffic accidents; hunting.

Status & conservation Non-native and locally common.

Population size & distribution GB population 52,000 (almost all in England; several hundred in Wales and fewer than 100 in Scotland). The population has increased continually over the last 25 years. In England, they have spread northward as far as Cheshire and Derbyshire. They are absent from Ireland.

Activity May be active at any time but feeds mainly in early morning, dusk and the middle of the day.

Dark scent glands are visible just beneath the eyes.

FIELD SIGNS

Runs and tunnels in undergrowth give a clue to the presence of muntjac. Males mark territories with small heaps of droppings and frayed stems where scent has been deposited. Droppings are nearly spherical or cylindrical pellets that are black and shiny, and sometimes pointed at one or both ends.

Footprints (slots) are about three centimetres long by two centimetres wide and one may be longer than the other.

Muntjacs have a repeated, loud, bark-like call that can continue for twenty minutes or more, but it can be confused with that of foxes.

Droppings are typically in piles of 20-120 pellets.

Roe deer *Capreolus capreolus*

Roe deer are native to Britain and are the most widespread deer in Britain. They are relatively small, about the size of a goat (their Latin name means 'little goat'), with a long neck and legs.

When disturbed they have a characteristic bounding gait and display the white-cream patch on their rump (called a caudal patch). In females, this patch is shaped like an inverted heart and has a white tuft at its base, while in males it is kidney-shaped and lacks the tuft. Like most small deer species, roe deer tend to be solitary.

Roe deer browse on the shoots, leaves and flowers of many garden plants to the annoyance of some gardeners, who might lose a prize bloom. They can jump or scramble over fences almost two metres high, so preventing them getting into gardens is difficult (see *Possible conflicts*, page 83).

KEY FEATURES

Appearance
Roe deer have a deep reddish-brown coat of short, sleek hairs in summer, which turns grey-brown in winter. During May and June, when the winter coat is moulted, they can look quite moth-eaten. They have a distinctive black nose and a white chin, commonly with a black chinstrap, and can be distinguished from muntjac by their upright stance and pointed ears. Males have short antlers with a maximum of three points and knobbly bases.

Shoulder height	Weight
63–69 cm	18–27 kg

Reproduction Roe deer mate from mid-July to the end of August (two or three months earlier than other deer in Britain) and females give birth, often to twins or triplets, in May or June the following year. Young (kids) are hidden separately in long grass while their mothers forage and rest a short distance away. They eat some vegetation from five to ten days but suckling continues for three months.

Lifespan Most die before seven or eight years; the maximum recorded age in the wild is 14 years for males and 18 for females.

Diet Brambles and deciduous shoots and leaves in summer; ivy, conifers, ferns and heather in winter. They are opportunistic feeders with a taste for exotic plants in gardens. In farmland, they feed mostly on cultivated crops, especially cereals.

Habitat They generally occur in woodland but are found in many urban and suburban sites such as parks, golf courses and rough ground where there is sufficient tree or scrub cover.

Predators Foxes are the main predator of kids; golden eagles and wildcats also prey on them.

Threats Roe deer are hunted for their meat. Where roe and muntjac deer co-exist, there is evidence that muntjacs compete more successfully than roe deer. Roe deer are involved in the majority of road traffic collisions with deer.

Status & conservation Native and widespread.

Population size & distribution GB population 500,000 (Scotland, 350,000; England, 150,000). After nearly becoming extinct in England during the nineteenth century, the population has continuously increased over the last 40 years. They are now present throughout much of England and have recently colonised parts of Wales, but are absent from Ireland, the Isle of Wight and most of the Scottish islands.

Activity They are active throughout the day and night, feeding for longest around dusk and dawn. In winter, they may rest for up to 60 per cent of the time.

FIELD SIGNS

Droppings and footprints are similar to those of muntjac and the two species can be difficult to tell apart. Slots of roe deer can be up to 4.5 cm long by 3.5 cm wide and may show the dew claws.

Otter *Lutra lutra*

Little over a generation ago, otters in Britain were close to extinction. Today, although still scarce, they are nudging their way into our towns and cities.

Traditionally, otters were killed to protect fish stocks, for sport and for their fur. Populations recovered from a low in the 1960s and '70s after the use of organchlorine pesticides on farms and hunting were banned (in the 1970s). As water quality has improved, otters have followed fish stocks back to many rivers, including those in urban centres. They have been recorded in Bristol, Birmingham and Manchester, in the Ouseburn in Newcastle upon Tyne, and in the River Lee in east London. In 2008, the Wildlife Trusts estimated that otters are established in at least 13 towns and cities.

The first wild otter, a young male, to be found in central London for over a century, albeit dead, was found in Wapping in September 2006 having probably travelled down the River Lee.

Otters are restless, playful and secretive mammals that spend most of their time along riverbanks. They are perfectly adapted to a semi-aquatic life: webbed feet and a long, muscular tail enable

KEY FEATURES

Appearance
Otters have a streamlined, dark-brown body (that appears black when wet) and a long, tapered tail. They have short legs and a broad muzzle with prominent whiskers. From a distance, they can be confused with mink, particularly as they are found in similar habitats, but otters are larger and swim with just their head and neck visible above the water, while mink swim with much more of their body exposed.

Head–body length	Tail length	Weight
59–110 cm (males are larger than females on average).	35–45 cm	7–11 kg

them to swim easily at about one metre per second and they can see as well underwater as above it, diving to catch small fish or to avoid danger. At night or in murky waters, they rely on their stiff, sensitive whiskers to detect prey. They are usually solitary in rivers and occupy large home ranges covering tens of kilometres.

Otters mark their territory with their droppings, known as spraints, which they leave at conspicuous sites along the water's edge, and surveys of these have been the main way that otter populations have been monitored. The spraints have an unusual sweet, musky smell that has been compared with the smell of jasmine tea.

Reproduction Mating occurs at any time of the year and females give birth to two or three cubs, usually between May and August. Newborn cubs are about 12 centimetres long but grow quickly and can swim at three months. They leave the protection of their mothers at 10-12 months and can breed at two years old.

Lifespan Typically three to four years; the oldest wild otter recorded was 16 years.

Diet Mostly fish such as eels, but also water birds, such as moorhens and ducks, frogs and rabbits.

Habitat A wide range of aquatic habitats including clean rivers, lakes and coastlines; less commonly, marshy areas.

Predators Few natural predators.

Threats Road traffic accidents; drowning in fish and lobster traps; and pollution such as oil and PCBs.

Status & conservation Native and localised. A species action plan for otters was produced in 1995 as part of the UK Biodiversity Action Plan and they are fully protected in the UK under Schedules 5 and

6 of the Wildlife and Countryside Act 1981. They are classified as Near Threatened on the IUCN Red List. Seventy-three sites have been designated Special Areas of Conservation (SACs) specifically for otters.

Population size & distribution GB population 10,300 (Scotland, 7,950; England, 1,600; Wales, 750). The population has continually increased over the last 25 years and their range is expanding in England. Between 2009 and 2011, otters were recorded in every English county.

Activity Mostly nocturnal in rivers, with main periods of activity after dusk and before dawn.

FIELD SIGNS

Spraints are used to scent-mark along regular runs, at obvious sites such as stones or tree stumps. They are often black, with a distinctive, pleasant smell (unlike that of mink scats, which have been described as 'evil-smelling') and vary in size and shape from a small blob or smear to cylinders up to 10 cm long that contain fur, bones and fish scales.

Dens (called 'holts') are usually a hole in the bank, overhung by vegetation. Slides into the water can sometimes be seen in wet mud or snow and seem to be a sign of play.

Tracks are around 6 cm in width and show four or five oval toe pads with a short claw.

Pine marten *Martes martes*

Loss of woodland meant that pine martens were scarce in many lowland areas of Great Britain and Ireland by 1800 and hunting and trapping by gamekeepers and further habitat loss through the nineteenth and early twentieth centuries worsened the decline. Today, they are still rare, but within their range, in northwest Scotland and parts of Ireland, they will make use of roof spaces and gardens in urban areas, tempted by an omnivorous palate.

Pine martens are members of the weasel (mustelid) family that also includes stoats, badgers, polecats, otters and mink. They are superbly adapted climbers and extremely agile, leaping up to four metres between tree branches and adept at landing on their feet, unhurt, from heights. It is on the ground, however, that they hunt, mostly at night, and will mark large territories with droppings, often in prominent places such as the tops of rocks. They are also strong swimmers. During the day, they rest on branches or in hollow trees, birds' nests, or in burrows amongst rocks.

KEY FEATURES

Appearance
Pine martens have dense, lustrous chocolate-brown fur and a distinctive creamy-yellow patch on their chest and throat. They have a weasel-like body-shape but are much larger with prominent rounded ears and a bushy tail.

Head–body length	Tail length	Weight
36–55 cm	20–25 cm	1.3–1.9 kg

Reproduction Mating occurs in late summer and females usually give birth to two kits or cubs in April or May the following year. The young are born naked and blind, their eyes opening at five to six weeks. They leave the den at about three months. Pine martens do not successfully breed until between two and three years old, which means that populations are slow to increase.

Lifespan In the wild, about a quarter will live longer than three years and some will survive 11-12 years. In captivity, they can live to 18 years.

Diet Mainly voles and mice, but also rabbits, small birds, birds' eggs, berries and insects. Close to houses, they will scavenge from bird tables and rubbish bins and they have been known to enjoy sweet foods such as strawberry jam and marmalade if given the opportunity.

Habitat Woodland or more open ground with pockets of tree or scrub cover. In Scotland, natal dens are often in the roof spaces of buildings.

Predators Fox and golden eagle may be their main predators.

Threats Habitat fragmentation.

Status & conservation Native, locally common in parts of Scotland but very rare in England in Wales. They are a priority species in the UK Biodiversity Action Plan and have been fully protected since 1988 under Schedule 5 of the Wildlife and Countryside Act 1981.

Population size & distribution Scotland, 3,500; fewer than 100 in either England or Wales. In Scotland, their distribution is mostly confined to the north-west, and the population is expanding into Grampian, Tayside, Central and Strathclyde regions. In England and Wales, records are concentrated to the north-west of the Humber-Severn axis and the population seems to be being maintained by breeding rather than new releases or escapes of captive individuals.

Activity Generally nocturnal in winter; often active before dawn and after dusk in summer.

FIELD SIGNS

Dens in buildings, such as lofts or sheds, might be indicated by a mound of droppings (scats); food remains, though, are rarely found at dens. Like other carnivores, pine martens will deposit scats in prominent places throughout their territory, such as the intersections of paths and low walls. Scats are usually black and 4-12 cm long by 1-1.5 cm in diameter; their shape depends on what has been eaten but might be twisted if fur or feathers are present. Fresh scats have a slightly sweet and fruity smell but this can be similar to that of fox or other mustelid scats.

Dens are often in inaccessible places; the abandoned cottage above was home to a female that nested in the chimney stack.

Red squirrel *Sciurus vulgaris*

Red squirrels are more arboreal than grey squirrels and rarely come down to the ground. Where they occur, red squirrels will make as much use of urban green spaces as greys do and can be encouraged to visit feeding stations by providing an aerial route with a thick, natural rope, for example.

Red squirrels can store little fat and need to eat regularly; up to four-fifths of the time that they are active is spent foraging and feeding, using their dextrous front feet to manipulate food. They are active throughout the winter and, during late summer and autumn, will cache tree seeds and conifer cones just below the soil surface to eat when food is scarce. Scent glands in their cheeks mark the food so that hoards can be found at a later date.

Red squirrels are solitary for much of the time but are known to share dreys, especially during winter and spring. Pecking orders are established between individuals and aggressive encounters are marked by tail flicking and foot stamping.

.

KEY FEATURES

Appearance
Red squirrels are a uniform brown colour, ranging from deep brown to a bright chestnut colour. In winter, their coats can be greyer, and they have characteristic long, ear tufts.

Head–body length	Tail length	Weight
18–24 cm	14–20 cm	250–300 g

Reproduction Litters of one to six kits are born from February to April and a second litter from May to July. The young are weaned by ten weeks and may stay with their mother over winter.

Lifespan Typically about three years in the wild; a few reach six or seven years.

Diet Pinecones, seeds, fruit, tree shoots, buds, flowers, berries, bark and lichens.

Habitat Generally large pine forests, usually over 50 hectares in size, but also other types of woodland and urban areas such as parks and gardens.

Predators Polecats, pine martens and wildcats, as well as raptors, such as buzzards and goshawks, and some owls.

Threats Competition with grey squirrels; loss of woodland habitat; and disease (squirrel poxvirus).

Status & conservation Native, but many current populations have a recent Scandinavian ancestry from introductions in the 1960s. It is classified as Near Threatened in England, Wales and Northern Ireland but is locally common in Scotland. It is a priority species in the UK Biodiversity Action Plan.

Population size & distribution GB population 161,000 in 1995 (England, 30,000; Scotland, 121,000; Wales, 10,000) but numbers in England and Wales now are likely to be smaller. The population has declined steadily since the introduction of the grey squirrel, in both its range and size. In southern England, isolated populations remain on Brownsea and Furzey islands (Dorset) and the Isle of Wight; and populations are present in Wales, Lancashire, North Yorkshire, Durham, Cumbria and Norfolk. It is abundant in large parts of Scotland but absent from most of the Scottish islands. Red squirrels were relatively common until the 1940s.

Activity Diurnal and active throughout the year; in summer, they are most active two to four hours after dawn and two to four hours before sunset.

FIELD SIGNS

Feeding signs include split hazelnuts and stripped bark (hanging in long spiral twists from the stem or at the base of a tree) where squirrels have fed on sap. Signs are indistinguishable from those of grey squirrels though.

Droppings are almost spherical, about 5-8 mm long, yellowish in summer and darker or black in winter.

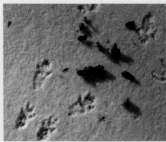

Hindfeet leave long prints, showing three narrow, central toes.

Shrews

Shrews are small insectivores (typically weighing less than a house mouse), akin to hedgehogs and moles. They are rarely seen as much of their time is spent beneath the leaf litter or in long vegetation but they are noisy, producing soft, high-pitched twitters while they forage and just-audible raucous shrieks and 'churls' in aggressive encounters with other shrews.

Three species of shrew occur in the built environment – common shrews, pygmy shrews and water shrews – and they are frequently the prey of domestic cats, accounting for about a fifth of mammals caught by the latter during the summer. An unpleasant-smelling secretion from shrews' scent glands, however, makes them unpalatable and few are actually eaten by cats. Unfortunately (for the shrew), there is no evidence that cats learn to avoid the musky scent, so it provides no protection – and there is little consolation in avoiding consumption once you are dead.

Shrew populations are largest in the summer when offspring are born but then shrink rapidly in the autumn as adults, less able to compete with younger individuals, die and juveniles disperse to establish their own territories.

Pygmy shrew

Common shrew *Sorex araneus*

Common shrews are one of Britain's most abundant mammals. They use a network of runways through the vegetation, digging burrows or using those of other small mammals. They forage with their snout and whiskers to probe and sniff out food and can locate prey up to 12 cm beneath the surface of the soil.

Shrews' small size means that they lose heat quickly and, in order to stay warm, they have a high metabolic rate. As a consequence, they must eat 80–90 per cent of their body weight in food each day (amounting to more than 500 prey) and small changes in the availability of food can threaten their survival.

They are solitary and aggressively defend their territories.

KEY FEATURES

Appearance
They have the distinctive narrow pointed snout of shrews and have brown (never black) fur on their back, with a paler, grey underside. The tails of adults tend to be bare and are often scarred.

Head–body length	Tail length	Weight
6–8 cm	About half the body length.	5–15 g

Reproduction Mating occurs between April and August. One or two litters of four to eight young are born from May onwards and females may have several litters in a season. The young sometimes caravan behind their mother during trips out of the nest, each grasping the tail of the one in front in its mouth, and are weaned by 25 days.

Lifespan In the wild, up to 15-18 months, but about half die before they reach two months and they are lucky to survive 12 months.

Diet Invertebrates such as earthworms, spiders, slugs, insect larvae and beetles, as well as carrion.

Habitat Shrews are found almost anywhere where there is ground cover. In urban environments they are found in the hedge bottoms and compost heaps of gardens, on road verges and grassy banks and are frequently found on derelict wasteland. More widely they are most abundant in thick grass, hedgerows and deciduous woodland. They make nests under logs and grass tussocks or in the burrows of other species.

Predators Domestic cats, owls and raptors, but also stoats, weasels and foxes.

Threats Habitat loss due to changes in farming practices, agricultural pesticides and pollution.

Status & conservation Native, widespread and common. A licence is necessary to trap and kill shrews.

Population size & distribution GB population 41,700,000. The population trend is unknown. They are found throughout Britain but are absent from Ireland, Shetland, Orkney, the Outer Hebrides, the Isle of Man, Isles of Scilly and Channel Islands.

Activity They are active during the day and night, although are most active during darkness. One- to two-hour bursts of activity are followed by periods of rest, usually in the nest but sometimes cat-napping elsewhere.

FIELD SIGNS

The most evident sign of shrews is their shrill calls, particularly during the breeding season, when encounters between individuals are marked by loud squeaks to warn off a rival .

Other signs, such as food remains or runways through leaf litter, are much less apparent, but owl pellets (such as that shown) can provide an indication that shrews are present in the area. Owl pellets contain the undigested remains of prey, such as parts of the skeleton and fur, which are coughed up by birds two or three times a day. The contents of pellets can be carefully separated in warm water. The jaw bones of common, water and pygmy shrews can be recognised by the red tips of the teeth.

Shrew remains are also sometimes found in discarded bottles which can trap small mammals.

Water shrew *Neomys fodiens*

Water shrews are well adapted to an aquatic lifestyle: they have denser, longer fur than that of terrestrial shrews and ears that can close in the water. A fringe of stiff silvery hairs runs the length of the underside of the tail, which they use as a rudder, and their hindfeet have similar fringes.

They can dive to depths of up to two metres and for up to 24 seconds, and while all shrews can swim, only water shrews hunt underwater as well as on land. They travel 50–150 metres along the water's edge each day to find food and shelter, and dig extensive networks of small burrows and chambers (lined with grass and leaves). The entrances to burrows are about two centimetres in diameter.

Like common and pygmy shrews, water shrews have teeth that are red-tipped, but unlike other species in Britain, they have venomous saliva that is capable of paralysing prey such as small fish and frogs.

KEY FEATURES

Appearance
Water shrews can be distinguished from other shrews by their black dorsal fur and larger size. Their tail is dark brown or black on top and they often have small white tufts on their ears.

Head–body length	Tail length	Weight
6–10 cm	5–8 cm – unlike common and pygmy shrews, water shrews' tails are almost as long as their body.	12–18 g

Reproduction Breeding extends through April to September, with a peak in May and June. One or two litters of 3-15 young are born each breeding season and some females may breed in their first calendar year. The young are weaned at about four weeks but stay with their mother for a further two weeks.

Lifespan 14–19 months; most adults die at the end of the breeding season.

Diet Mainly freshwater crustaceans such as shrimps, caddis-fly larvae and small snails, but also small fish, frogs and earthworms.

Habitat Mainly the banks of fast-flowing, clear, unpolluted water, but also lakes, reed-beds, fens and marshes. They are often found in man-made habitats including gardens and watercress beds.

Predators Occasionally owls, kestrels, foxes, large fish and cats.

Threats Habitat loss through water pollution and the intensive management of watercourses.

Status & conservation Native and locally common.

Population size & distribution GB population 1,900,000. The population trend is unknown but numbers are possibly declining. Water shrews are widely distributed in mainland Britain, particularly in central and southern England. They are scarce in the Scottish Highlands and absent from Ireland and the Isle of Man, and most of the small islands.

Activity They are active throughout the year and are mostly nocturnal. They are particularly active just before dawn.

FIELD SIGNS

The remains of prey, such as snail shells or the cases of caddis larvae, can often be found at a favourite feeding spot, such as on top of a stone.

Burrow entrances, in the banks of streams, rivers and drainage ditches, are rounded and about 2 cm in diameter; unlike those of bank voles, there is little disturbance of vegetation around them.

Pygmy shrews *(Sorex minutus)* are one of Britain's smallest mammals – only pipistrelle bats weigh as little. During the summer, when they breed, they can be up to 10 g in weight, but are typically 3.5-7 g, between that of a one and two pence coin. They have grey-brown fur, paler than that of the common shrew, and a long, slightly hairy tail. Pygmy shrews are active both day and night, but rest frequently. They use a network of runways like common shrews but do not dig for prey beneath the soil surface and never eat earthworms, which are probably too large to tackle.

Pygmy shrews consume one and a quarter times their body weight each day in order to maintain their energetic metabolisms, and beetles, spiders and woodlice make up most of their diet. They are solitary and territorial and emit a high-pitched squeak or swipe their tail from side to side in encounters with other pygmy shrews.

They are one of two species of shrew found in Ireland; the other – the greater white-toothed shrew – was reported there for the first time in 2008.

Stoats and weasels

Stoats and weasels are only rarely found in urban areas, but might be spotted at sites near to a rabbit warren or around grain or timber stores that support thriving populations of small mammals. Stoats and weasels are well adapted to pursuing prey into burrows: they have a sleek, sinuous shape and are exceptionally inquisitive. They are fierce predators and will kill and carry prey much larger than themselves, but are graceful and extraordinary animals to watch.

Stoat

Stoat *Mustela erminea*

Stoats are very playful creatures with an insatiable curiosity; they tirelessly explore holes, buildings and even people, if they sense that there is no danger. While foraging, they 'periscope' – standing upright on their hind legs – to gain a better view of their surroundings and will check every available burrow and crevice for food. They are excellent swimmers and climbers, and will raid birds' nests, nest boxes and squirrel dreys.

Stoats (and weasels) are known for a strange behaviour that supposedly mesmerises their prey: they cavort about, twisting and leaping, to draw curious prey nearer. When they are close enough, the hapless prey are seized. However, an alternative explanation for the behaviour is that it is due to the irritation caused by a parasite that infects the sinuses of stoats and weasels; whether it is a hunting strategy or due to the parasite is still unknown.

KEY FEATURES

Appearance
Stoats are typically a more sandy-brown colour than weasels but can be a similar chestnut brown. They have a yellowish-white underside and a black-tipped tail, which bristles in moments of excitement (the tails of weasels are shorter and uniformly coloured). In Scotland, Wales and the west of England, some stoats turn snow-white in winter, with only the tip of the tail remaining black. Elsewhere, their winter coat can be piebald or remain brown.

Head–body length	Tail length	Weight
18–32 cm	7–12 cm	100–445 g

Reproduction Stoats mate during the summer and females produce a single litter of 6-13 kittens (or kits) the following spring. Females kits are sexually mature at two to three weeks and are mated with before they are weaned, by males that enter the nest. Young stoats develop rapidly and are able to hunt for themselves at about 11 weeks old.

Lifespan Up to three or four years in the wild and very rarely six to eight years.

Diet Mainly rabbits and small rodents, but also birds and occasionally rats, squirrels and shrews.

Habitat Stoats will live in most places where there is sufficient cover and food, including woodland, cultivated land, hilly areas and grassland.

Predators Foxes, owls, kestrels and occasionally cats.

Threats Stoats are legally trapped and shot by gamekeepers because they kill game birds.

Status & conservation Native, common and widespread.

Population size & distribution GB population 462,000. The population has continually increased over the last 25 years. Stoats are widely distributed throughout Britain and Ireland, though only rarely in urban areas.

Activity Stoats may be active at any time, but tend to be mainly nocturnal in winter and diurnal in summer.

FIELD SIGNS

Signs of weasels and stoats are difficult to find. Scats are thin and twisted, and usually contain fur or feathers. The scats of weasels are 3-6 cm long and those of stoats, 4-8 cm long. Occasionally, individual scats are found on prominent stones or in the middle of tracks.

Weasel nests are sometimes found under corrugated iron sheets left on grassland and in collapsed stone walls, and may be marked by half-eaten prey remains.

Weasel *Mustela nivalis*

Weasels are Britain's smallest carnivores. They hunt along hedgerows or stonewalls, investigating each hollow and burrow. Like stoats, weasels stand up on their hind legs, surveying their surroundings for smells and any movement. In early summer, family groups can sometimes be seen together, made up of a female and her offspring, learning to hunt. Adults, though, hunt alone and stories of marauding gangs of weasels in tales such as *The Wind in the Willows*, are just that – tales.

Their small size means that weasels must eat a third of their body weight each day and when prey is scarce, their numbers can fall sharply. In bad years (with few rodent prey), populations can become locally extinct, but they are good at recolonising areas and, when conditions improve, populations quickly return.

KEY FEATURES

Appearance
Weasels are smaller than stoats and have a whiter belly (the line between the dark and lighter fur is irregular rather than straight as it is in stoats). Their tails are proportionally shorter than those of stoats and lack the black bushy tip.

Head–body length	Tail length	Weight
17–25 cm (males are larger than females).	3–6 cm	48–195 g

Reproduction Mating occurs between April and July and a litter of four or five kits is born in April or May the following year. When food is plentiful, a second litter may be born in July or August, and those born earlier in the year may themselves produce offspring. As a result, populations are quick to recover if numbers have fallen. Kits are weaned after three to four weeks and hunting behaviour is developed by eight weeks.

Lifespan Up to two years.

Diet Mainly mice and voles, but also rabbits, small birds and eggs in spring.

Habitat Almost anywhere that provides enough cover and prey, including sand dunes, farmland, grassland and woodland.

Predators Foxes, owls, kestrels and cats.

Threats They are also killed by gamekeepers, although traps are most often set for stoats, which are more of a threat to game birds.

Status & conservation Native, common and widespread.

Population size & distribution GB population 450 000. The population has continually increased over the last 25 years. Weasels are widely distributed across Britain but absent from Ireland and some offshore islands, including the Isle of Man and the Channel Islands.

Activity Mostly diurnal.

Telling weasels and stoats apart

The most distinctive feature distinguishing weasels and stoats is the bushy black tip of the latter's tail, which weasels lack. The head and body length of an adult stoat is greater than the length of a house brick, while weasels are usually shorter, and stoats have proportionately longer tails, around a third of their head and body length, compared with less than a quarter for weasels.

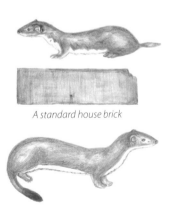

A standard house brick

Both stoats and weasels are chestnut brown in colour with a paler underside. In stoats, the line demarcating the dark fur of the back and paler ventral fur is straight, whereas in weasels it is irregular.

In Ireland, the absence of weasels makes the problem of identification much simpler.

Yellow-necked mouse *Apodemus flavicollis*

Yellow-necked mice are woodland specialists but, if the opportunity is there, they move into houses with surprising regularity. In Britain, they are found only in southern England and Wales but, even where they do occur, they can be rare.

Yellow-necked mice are similar in appearance and behaviour to wood mice and it was only in 1894 that the two were identified as separate species. Yellow-necked mice can be identified by a complete, yellow 'collar' of fur between their front legs (shown on the right, below); in contrast, the yellow chest-patch of wood mice never joins the dark brown fur on either side of their neck.

Yellow-necked mice are good climbers, travelling large distances in trees to forage. They make use of extensive burrow systems, mostly within half a metre of the surface and often between tree roots or under fallen timber. Burrows are frequently used to store seeds and invertebrate prey. Yellow-necked mice are more tolerant of each other than wood mice: three or four adults may nest together and there is evidence that long-term pair bonds form between mates.

KEY FEATURES

Appearance
Yellow-necked mice are slightly larger than wood mice and their fur is more orange in colour; their bellies are a brighter white than those of wood mice.

Head–body length	Tail length	Weight
10–12 cm	Longer than body.	22–56 g

Yellow-necked mice are found most frequently in houses between October and March, occupying roof and wall spaces in about half of instances. Why they enter, though, is not known. It is unlikely to be in search of food, as their natural diet of seeds is most abundant at that time of year; similarly, elsewhere in Europe they withstand very cold winters, so it is unlikely that they are escaping the cold.

Reproduction Up to three litters of 4-11 pups are born each year between February and October. The young are weaned by four weeks. Those born in the spring are sexually mature at about ten weeks and can breed in the same calendar year; autumn-born offspring usually reproduce only in the following spring.

Lifespan Few survive longer than 12 months.

Diet Similar foods to wood mice but specialising on tree seeds; their diet is broadest in spring, when seedlings, buds and insect larvae are eaten.

Habitat Mainly deciduous and mixed woodland, but occasionally mature hedgerows, cereal fields and other habitats. They prefer areas with good canopy cover. In winter, they enter houses from nearby woodland, as well as garages and outbuildings, and individuals will use roadside verges.

Predators Barn and tawny owls, stoats, weasels, badgers, foxes and domestic cats.

Threats Loss of mature woodland habitat.

Status & conservation Native and locally common.

Population size & distribution GB population 750,000. The population trend is unknown. Yellow-necked mice are common only in the south and south-east of England, and central Wales. Records from Neolithic and Roman sites suggest that they were once more widespread than they are now. They are absent from Scotland and Ireland.

Activity Nocturnal.

FIELD SIGNS

Field signs of yellow-necked mice are identical to those of wood mice; droppings are the most apparent sign.

Nests are sometimes located above ground and might, as in this case, be in disused birds' nests.

Urban habitats

Diverse, linked spaces

The average size of the 16 million gardens in Britain is around 160 square metres (equivalent to an area 42 feet by 42 feet). The home ranges of most mammals – the areas that they regularly occupy – are a lot larger than this and, for gardens and urban green spaces to support mammals, a network of sites has to be accessible; it has to be possible to move from one to another. Biologists talk of 'fragmented' habitats and 'connectivity' – the ease with which wildlife can move between different areas of habitat.

Birds have free passage; even if the environment is patchy, they can move easily between one resource-rich patch and another. Mammals, travelling on foot, on the other hand, have to overcome obstacles such as walls and fences, concreted areas and roads. The distance between sites is important too: small mammals such as wood mice might disperse no further than 600 metres in urban areas.

Because moving between urban sites can be difficult, an important characteristic of these spaces for mammals is that they are made up of lots of different, smaller-scale habitats (microhabitats) that separately meet different requirements. Urban green spaces are best when they pack a lot in. Gardens make up between a fifth and a quarter of urban areas. They are far from uniform and there are opportunities even in small spaces to cultivate habitats and build features that, on a neighbourhood scale, are good for mammals.

Microhabitats

Trees and shrubs

The feature of gardens most strongly linked to a rich invertebrate fauna (that will feed most small mammals) is the abundance of trees taller than two metres. Growing tall vegetation, such as shrubs, hedges and trees, is the most important single thing gardeners can do to encourage biodiversity. As well as the invertebrates that live or feed directly on trees, others make use of the shade or leaf litter that tall shrub and tree species provide. Invertebrates are prey for nearly all urban mammals: bats feed almost exclusively on insects, such as moths, beetles and flies; insects and earthworms make up a half or more of the foods consumed by hedgehogs and badgers; a quarter of those eaten by foxes; and a substantial part of the diet of wood mice and brown rats.

In spring, many mammal species feed on buds and fruit blossoms and, in autumn, on ripe berries and fruit. Hazel *(Corylus avellana)*, crab-apple *(Malus sylvestris)*, hawthorn *(Crataegus monogyna)* and wayfaring tree *(Viburnum lantana)* are all beneficial to small mammals.

Trees provide a three-dimensional habitat, exploited best by squirrels, but ground cover – such as bramble or bundles of branches – is also important for many small mammals. Bank voles, for example, will benefit if areas of cover are left when clearing patches of ground. In addition, mature trees provide summer roosts for Daubenton's bats and pipistrelles.

Hedges

Hedges mimic a woodland edge, providing an element of shelter and protection, and species such as rowan *(Sorbus aucuparia)*, hornbeam *(Carpinus betulus)* and wild cherry *(Prunus avium)* provide fruits and foliage that wood mice, bank voles and rabbits feed on.

The overgrown base of a hedge provides summer and winter nest sites for hedgehogs and, importantly, hedges can act as green corridors between gardens, providing access to and connecting green spaces.

Hawthorn (Crataegus monogyna): *scented white flowers in spring are followed by glossy red haws later in the year.*

Lawns

Lawns frequently make up a large part of a garden's area (on average, around three-fifths of the area of gardens in the BUGS project). Much of the cover provided by a lawn comes from grasses, but the majority of plant-types in a lawn are other species, making these areas surprisingly species-rich. Lawns are more similar to semi-natural grassland than to cultivated flower beds and borders and, when mown, are ideal foraging habitats for hedgehogs and badgers.

There is more to lawns than grasses: the BUGS project recorded 159 species (other than mosses, lichens and liverworts) in 52 garden lawns; and flowers such as white clover (*Trifolium repens*), self-heal (*Prunella vulgaris*) and bird's-foot trefoil (*Lotus corniculatus*) will support insects, including butterfly, bee and hoverfly species. Larvae of several species feed on the roots of lawn plants such as daisies and plantains, and it is these that species such as badgers forage for.

Rat-tail plantain

When the soil is hard, however, hunting soil invertebrates is difficult and dry summers can be lean times for hedgehogs, badgers and fox cubs. Watering the lawn in the evening (just before these species begin foraging and when the ground is less likely to dry out) keeps earthworms and insect larvae near the surface where they are caught more easily.

Long grass

While short grass provides a good foraging habitat for hedgehogs and others, leaving the edges of a lawn to grow taller provides cover for voles and sites for hedgehogs to nest during the summer. Typically, hedgehogs build less structured nests in the summer than they do as hibernacula and, if the weather is warm, they sometimes simply lie hidden in long grass or under leaves.

Yellow rattle *(Rhinanthus minor)* or wild carrot *(Daucus carota)* sown in autumn around the edges of a lawn provide taller plants giving cover to hedgehogs and field voles.

Compost heaps and wood piles

Compost heaps resemble a forest-floor habitat where decaying material accumulates. They support invertebrates and fungi, provide shelter and food for mammals, and hibernation sites for hedgehogs (and other vertebrates, such as slow-worms and frogs).

Stick and log piles are excellent habitats as well. Around 900 invertebrate species live in or on dead wood in Britain, many in urban environments. Logs around ten centimetres in diameter provide sufficient gaps between each other for invertebrates to exploit. Partially burying the wood or covering the pile in grass cuttings or dead leaves prevents the habitat drying out. Wood mice frequently use wood piles to nest under.

Wood habitats can be created by leaving tree stumps in situ to rot down or by piling logs and tree branches in a shady corner of the garden. Log piles can be held in place with posts, or logs buried singularly or in groups, to a depth of about 50 cm.

Ponds

Digging a pond is an excellent way to encourage (and appreciate) wildlife in gardens – provided a little thought is given to mammals. Ponds can be watering-holes (particularly important in dry weather) and sources of invertebrates and amphibians that are on the menu of many mammals; but they can also be a hazard: one survey in London that recorded dead hedgehogs found that nearly ten per cent had drowned. Hedgehogs are good swimmers, but steep-sided ponds can make it is impossible for them to climb out and they can drown, exhausted. Small strips of chicken wire hung over the edge into the water or a small pile of bricks built up in the corner of a pond provide a means of escape.

Rockeries and walls

Rockeries mimic bare rock and scree habitats, providing sites for insects and reptiles to sunbathe, nesting sites for solitary bees and wasps, and hibernation sites for frogs and toads. Field voles and wood mice nest and breed under stones and in dry walls, and brown rats and wood mice will forage in climbing plants covering walls.

Domestic mammals

Some mammals, those we keep as livestock or pets, we deliberately place in the built environment and one in particular, a medium-sized predator that we share our homes with, is a significant feature of the urban landscape for wild mammals.

Cats *(Felis catus)* have gone one better than many mammal species: rather than adopting, to a lesser or greater extent, an urban lifestyle, cats have adopted us. The skeleton of a kitten buried alongside a person 9,500 years ago in Cyprus is the earliest evidence of an association between cats and people. All domestic cats today are descended from African wildcats *(Felis silvestris lybica)* that began their own domestication in the Near East around the time that people began storing grain and attracting rodents, perhaps 12,000 years ago.

Domestic cats (Felis catus) *are the most abundant carnivores in Britain; of about nine million cats, around a tenth are feral.*

They reached Britain from the eastern Mediterranean with the Romans, and around nine million domestic cats prowl Britain today, predominantly in towns and cities.

For the most part, we willingly share our homes with cats not for their services as mousers but as companions. Even so, we live with formidable predators and typically there might be more than 200 in a square urban kilometre. From records of the prey that cats bring home, one study estimated that around 60 million mammals are caught by cats nationally between the start of April and the end of August (twice the number of birds caught); across the whole year (and given that not all the prey caught will be brought back), the figure is likely to be twice that.

Wild mammals, such as hedgehogs, can benefit from food (for example, tinned cat food) put out at night and do not become reliant on hand-outs or stop foraging normally. Feeding might be particularly important for individuals born at the end of the summer who have little time to put on sufficient weight for hibernation.

Wood mice are the most commonly caught prey, followed by rabbits, voles and shrews, and, for wood mice at least, predation by cats might be the main factor limiting their numbers. Cat owners can make some redress though: cats that wear bells or that are kept indoors at night catch fewer mammals (although the same number of birds) as those without a bell or that are let out at night, reducing the impact on small mammal populations.

Improving our lot

Actions to improve gardens and other urban spaces for wildlife need not be on a grand scale. Creating different microhabitats, even within the smallest garden, and encouraging biodiversity is key. Building a log pile or compost heap, leaving an undisturbed corner to grow wild or putting out some food can all be attractions for mammals, and welcoming wild neighbours in enriches our towns and cities for everyone.

Possible conflicts

Inevitably, there are occasions when the attentions of wild residents are not welcomed; gardens, allotments, cemeteries and recreational areas have functions other than as habitats for wildlife and, when the two conflict, hackles can be raised. But in gardens and allotments at least, away from ornamental lawns or plant nurseries, a compromise can be reached with a measure of tolerance. It is difficult to selectively keep out a single species, but most can be discouraged and an acknowledgement that it is a matter of give and take – shouldering some inconvenience for the benefits of seeing a wild mammal close to – is the best policy.

Moles

Moles are a remarkable mammal but, for one that few people have ever seen, they attract an extraordinary amount of ill-will. The molehills that mark the spoils of their labour are seen as a nuisance and moles have received short shrift from gardeners. But molehills are not all bad news.

In gardens, lawns tend to show the brunt of moles' handiwork and gardeners have waged a largely fruitless war for centuries against the animals responsible. It is doubtful, though, that the amount of the damage justifies the measures that are used to control them. Neither kill-traps – such as 'scissor' (e.g. Talpex) or 'half-tunnel' (Duffus) traps – nor gassing (with phosphine) are always humane. The array of deterrents available, from the high-tech to the homespun, has mixed success, and none wins plaudits from everybody – or even from a majority of users.

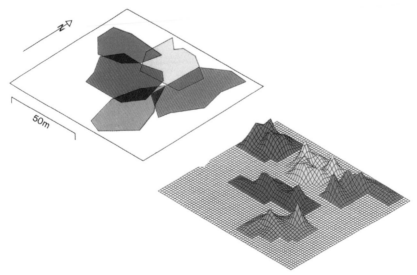

The tunnel systems of male moles may overlap with several females, and those of females overlap with other females (shown by the overlapping coloured areas, top). The tunnels of neighbouring moles are sometimes interconnected but residents tend to avoid confrontation. The tunnels occupied most are indicated by the highest peaks (in the bottom diagram); shared territory is used by only one individual at a time. After the death or removal of a mole from its burrow, neighbouring moles quickly annex the vacant tunnels, often within 24 hours. (Plots produced by Martyn L. Gorman.)

Sonic devices, which create vibrations through the soil, and their low-tech counterparts (such as toy windmills or half-sunken bottles), have their supporters and detractors alike, but at least one study, which radio-tracked moles, has shown mechanical devices have no effect at all. Putting the contributions of a pet dog or cat in mole runs probably has fewer fans – the intention is that the smell of a large predator will deter the mole's approach. Alternatively, the similar use of garlic or elder twigs has been suggested, and claims have been made for alliums and plants such as stinking hellebore *(Hellesborus foetidus)*, crown imperial *(Fritillaria imperialis)* and castor oil plant *(Ricinus communis)* as repellents.

For most, moles pose little problem: soil heaps are easily cleared away, avoiding an invasion of weeds, and damage to growing plants is only temporary. Moreover, killing or live-trapping and removing moles is unlikely to be effective – other moles move in to empty territories and may exacerbate the situation by extending existing tunnels. Instead, the best policy is to put moles to good use.

Most of the soil pushed up into molehills comes from beneath the seed bank (the top few inches of soil that contains dormant weed seeds) and, after the birds have been at it, it is largely free of insect larvae. The textured soil is excellent for potting plants.

Moles will feed on troublesome species such as leatherjackets (crane fly larvae), chafer larvae and wireworm (click beetle larvae), which can damage lawns, and their tunnels can help to aerate the soil. Tunnels can also help drainage, although moles tend to avoid wet soils.

Deer

Roe deer and muntjac are predominantly browsers (rather than grazers), feeding on the shoots, leaves and flowers of many garden plants and deciduous trees. Like most species of small deer, they tend to be solitary, so any damage is likely to be limited to the attentions of a single individual or, at most, two or three animals at any one time.

Foxgloves (Digitalis), *left;* lavender *(Lavandula),* top; *and* Berberis, *above, tend to be avoided by deer.*

Excluding deer from gardens is difficult: muntjac will push under fences and through small holes, and roe deer can jump or scramble over fences almost two metres in height. As a guide, fencing 1.5 metres high is recommended for muntjac and 1.9 metres for roe deer, and it is best to avoid plastic netting, which risks entangling deer and other animals. Plastic spirals offer little protection to saplings; tree guards should be at least 1.2 metres high.

A combination of protecting the most vulnerable plants and growing species that deer tend to avoid is probably the best course. *Berberis*, lavender *(Lavandula)*, coloneasters, foxgloves *(Digitalis)* and rosemary *(Rosmarinus officinalis)* are usually low on their preferred menu.

Foxes

Most complaints about foxes to local authorities are made either during the breeding season in late January and early February when foxes are most vocal, or from late April to August when cubs are growing up. Complaints, however, are from a minority: for most people a litter of cubs under a shed or playing in and flattening a flowerbed or vegetable patch is not a nuisance; for many it is a bonus to see a wild carnivore up close.

The smell of fertilisers containing animal remains (such as fish, blood or bonemeal) may attract foxes (and badgers) to gardens; avoiding the use of these will help not to encourage animals in. Foxes do scavenge from rubbish bins but it is a lot rarer than generally thought. Wheelie bins are completely fox-proof and putting a heavy lid on a conventional bin is sufficient to prevent foxes from raiding it.

Two safe, scent repellents, *Scoot* and *Get Off My Garden*, are available. Traditionally used repellents such as creosote, diesel and Renardine are hazards in themselves and should not be used.

Badgers

As urban areas continue to expand, badgers can become unwitting town-dwellers. Even in new surroundings, however, they can insist on the right of way. Badgers stick to a network of paths that lead to foraging areas and between the entrances of a sett (which might have been occupied for tens or even hundreds of years). When these established routes meet a man-made obstacle, such as a road or a stone wall, badgers will often just keep going.

In Britain, road traffic is the single largest cause of deaths in badgers, accounting for perhaps a half of fatalities of adults and cubs that have emerged from the sett. When new roads cross established badger paths, accidents are particularly common.

In gardens, a large, opportunistic omnivore, with strong limbs adapted for digging, can cause considerable upheaval. Lawns can be dug up in search of earthworms and insect larvae; fruit trees damaged; and root vegetables unearthed. More rarely, excavations by badgers can undermine buildings. But badgers are not a threat to either people or pets and, unless injured or trapped, will almost always move away.

It is possible to build a fence that will stop badgers getting into your garden, but they can easily break through or dig under a poorly constructed fence and, if it prevents a badger from moving to or from its sett, it may be a legal offence. A strong wooden fence (at least 120 centimetres high) with wire mesh attached and extending (at least 60 centimetres) below ground is necessary. Alternatively, gaps or gates along regular paths can be put in, minimising any damage to fences. Badger gates are heavy enough to prevent small dogs pushing through but allow badgers access.

Badgers in Your Garden produced by the Badger Trust is a good source of information and can be downloaded at: http://www.badger.org.uk.

Rabbits

Rabbits feed primarily on grasses but their catholic tastes take in vegetables, ornamental flowers, shrubs, fruit bushes and trees. There is no guaranteed method to prevent rabbits from feeding on garden or allotment plants: enclosing beds in rabbit-proof fencing is probably the best option. Fencing needs to be one metre high and, if made out of wire-mesh, with a mesh size no larger than 30 millimetres (young rabbits can squeeze through a gap of 35 millimetres and adults can get through spaces in chain-link fencing). Rabbits are adept burrowers and it is necessary to sink the fence to a depth of 30 centimetres to deter them from getting underneath. Traditionally, dried gorse or holly leaves were used to surround areas, or a border of rue *(Ruta graveolens)* planted. It might be tempting to fence the whole garden, but this excludes other species too.

Alternatively, plants that rabbits naturally tend to avoid can be brought centre-stage: snowdrops *(Galanthus)* and daffodils *(Narcissus)* in spring, and flowers such as yellow flag *(Iris pseudacorus)*, cyclamen and foxgloves *(Digitalis)*. Berry-producing plants too, in general, tend to be avoided. A more prosaic measure for deterring rabbits – based on the premise that rabbits tend not to feed around cow pats – suggests spraying areas with liquid manure.

Urban surveys

Finding out what's there

Mammals for the most part are not a showy lot: most are crepuscular or nocturnal; some, such as wood mice, shrews, voles and rabbits, are meals for others or for raptors, and do their best to keep out of sight. So surveying mammals is not an easy business. But knowing how a population is faring – how its range and size is changing over a long period – is essential to a species' conservation or to its management. Collecting populations' vital statistics means it is possible to assess what needs to be done and whether conservation efforts are working.

A species distribution might encompass most of the British Isles, making any survey a herculean task, and the built environment, despite being on our doorstep, presents its own challenges. Much of the urban landscape is made up of numerous small, private gardens and to understand how these and other spaces support wildlife needs a willing army of volunteers, each to survey their own patch. Luckily, such an army exists: the collective efforts of volunteers in surveys of mammals in Britain have been estimated to amount to over 140,000 hours each year, at over 16,500 sites.

All this has a monetary value but, in practice, such 'citizen science' is invaluable: monitoring wild mammals over much of their range could not be done any other way.

The importance of monitoring

Surveys gather information about where species occur (their range) and the numbers of individuals (the size of a population). Each survey is a snapshot of a population at a particular instant – in the month or season that the survey was carried out or over an individual year. But to understand how a population is changing, repeated surveys are needed, and to identify the long-term 'health' of a population, repeated surveys over several years are necessary. In that way, underlying trends can be spotted.

Wild populations change in size over a single year and from one year to the next, and underlying trends – the tendency of a population to grow, for example, or to remain the same size – can be obscured by these regular variations over shorter timescales. The number of wood mice, for example, triples in autumn, after offspring are born; and, in years when there is abundant tree seed (in woodland habitats), more individuals survive the winter, bolstering the population the following spring. Vole populations too can show yearly variations in size, peaking in autumn or early winter; and those of field voles in some areas of Britain cycle with peaks every three to four years, possibly because of changes in the abundance or quality of food, or the spread of infections.

But conservation is concerned with underlying trends – and even then, populations can change very quickly.

Red squirrels were not an unusual sight in many places sixty years ago, although the population had decreased since the start of the century. Today, there are fewer than 30,000 in England and they survive in only a handful of areas. Black rats similarly were still commonly seen in the major ports and in towns along the network of canals in the middle of the last century. In 1942, black rats were found in 21 per cent of the buildings (mainly warehouses) in the Port of London, compared with 16 per cent that were inhabited by brown rats. And, of 1,020 rats that were killed in the Port that year, four-fifths were black rats – almost as many as make up the whole population in England, Scotland and Wales today. Changes in dockyards, though, with the introduction of containerised shipping and the storage of foodstuffs in silos, have meant that ports are no longer a stronghold for black rats. In the time between one generation and its grandchildren it is clear that a species can all but disappear.

It is also true that populations can recover just as quickly and the fortunes of otters are one of those on the up. In the 1970s, otters were absent from much of England; forty years later, they have been recorded in every English county and, in the fifth national survey of otters in 2009-10, the proportion of sites showing evidence of otters was ten-fold greater than that in the first survey in 1977-79.

Conservationists are mindful that populations can disappear before you know it – and, if actions are going to be taken to preserve them, it is necessary to keep track of how a species is faring.

Surveys of urban habitats

A thriving community of mammals is an indicator of a 'healthy' environment. The green spaces, soil and trees that support the invertebrate prey of species such as bats, shrews and hedgehogs, for example, are also those that cycle nutrients, drain rainwater, reduce air pollution and support pollinators, which support the human residents of urban areas.

Four surveys currently record mammals in specifically urban habitats: one – the *English House Condition Survey* – only collects records of house mice and brown rats; and two (run separately by the RSPB and the British Trust for Ornithology) were set up primarily

If mammal species are doing well, then the species that they feed on – moths (such as the noctuid in the mouth of the pipistrelle, above), flies, ground beetles, earthworms and slugs – are likely to be thriving too.

to record bird species. The BTO's *Garden BirdWatch* and People's Trust for Endangered Species' *Living with Mammals* are the only two surveys that have run over a long enough period to identify population trends of mammals in urban areas.

Living with Mammals

In its first nine years, over 1,900 volunteers have taken part in *Living with Mammals* surveying 2,500 separate sites in Britain and submitting 5,500 survey forms. Over 130,000 records of sightings or field signs have been collected since it began, identifying 24 species or groups of species. Around four-fifths of sites are private gardens but the remainder include the other types of spaces – allotments, railway embankments, golf courses and others – that make up the built landscape.

The survey defines the built environment as areas within 200 metres of buildings. Sites such as those in small villages or rural areas adjacent to farm buildings are included even though they are not 'urban' in a strict sense. They are, however, areas where people work or live and whose importance to wildlife might be overlooked. Overall, the distribution of survey sites matches that of built land, indicating that most of the sites in the survey are urban or suburban.

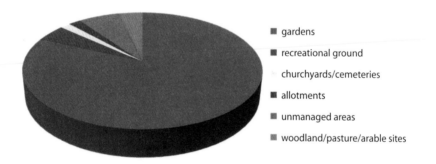

■ gardens

■ recreational ground

churchyards/cemeteries

■ allotments

■ unmanaged areas

■ woodland/pasture/arable sites

Most of the sites surveyed in Living with Mammals *are gardens but around a fifth are other types of green space, reflecting the diversity of habitats in urban areas. Common ground, derelict sites, railway embankments and river banks are shown as 'unmanaged areas' in the chart.*

Different types of site support different species and vary in the number and abundance of species that are present. Analysing thousands of records shows that gardens score highest and are home to between three and four wild mammal species on average. Common ground, golf courses, playing fields and waste land score well too, while churchyards, allotments, parks, and roadside verges and railway embankments have the lowest number.

Another apparent difference is in how different species are faring – how their populations are changing in the long-term. The graphs (opposite) show the proportion of sites that recorded foxes and moles in each year of the *Living with Mammals* survey (shown as blue squares). Foxes and moles tend to ruffle human feathers: rather than being seen as intelligent, adaptable wild cousins of our cherished pet dogs and extraordinary, subterranean insectivores, they tend to be demonised for minor misdemeanours, and perennial claims of escalating numbers are regularly announced in the media. The only problem is that such claims are not based on evidence from surveys, and the data that exist describe a different picture. In urban areas at least, the proportion of sites recording moles each year and that record foxes, show trends (red lines) that are neither up nor down. The figure one year might be higher or lower than that for the previous year but, over the period as a whole, the picture is of a stable population. The only way to

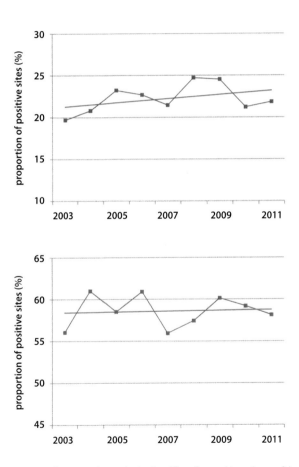

The proportion of sites recording moles (top) and foxes (bottom) in each year of the Living with Mammals *survey (blue squares). Indications of population trends are shown by the red lines, suggesting populations of the two species in urban areas are changing little in the long-term.*

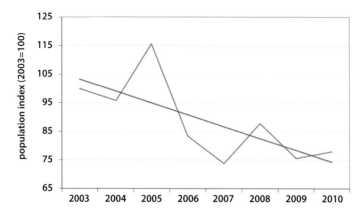

The population trend (red) of hedgehogs in an analysis of the Living with Mammals *data. Over eight years of the survey, the trend fell by 32 per cent. The blue line shows the year-to-year change in a measure of the population relative to that in the first year of the survey.*

know how a wild population is changing is by repeated surveys and sound science. Unsupported claims are not a basis on which to plan conservation actions or manage wild populations.

In contrast to that for foxes or moles, the evidence for hedgehogs is a bigger cause for concern. Using the records from sites that took part more than once, a measure (or *index*) of the population can be calculated (analysing only these sites means that population changes can be detected more easily). Between 2003 and 2010, the population trend for hedgehogs fell by 4.7 per cent each year, a decrease of almost a third over the eight years (above).

Living with Mammals is not the only survey to show this downward trend.

BTO *Garden BirdWatch*

The British Trust for Ornithology has been running volunteer-based surveys of birds since the 1930s and more recently it has branched out to include non-feathered species. In 2003, its *Garden BirdWatch* survey began collecting records of mammals and, in 2010, records were submitted from over 3,000 gardens.

Between 2007 (when records started to be collected online) and 2010, nearly 25,000 records of hedgehogs were submitted by one in three of those collecting records of mammals. Over that period, the population trend fell by over a third (36 per cent).

These two surveys have provided the first strong evidence that hedgehog numbers are declining in urban areas, as well as in the wider landscape, and have put a figure on the speed with which hedgehogs are disappearing. Volunteers getting involved in recording schemes and sharing their experience and enthusiasm make the science possible and they might just be the saving grace for hedgehogs too.

The combination of habitats in gardens can suit hedgehogs down to the ground: lawns provide an ideal foraging habitat and compost heaps, herbaceous borders and hedges can provide shelter. Urban gardens and other green spaces could be a haven for hedgehog populations threatened in rural areas. However, the average size of a garden in Britain is about 160 square metres and the home ranges of hedgehogs are at least five hectares for females and three times that for males – a lot larger than any individual garden. Hedgehogs typically travel a kilometre in a night, so conservation needs to be on a neighbourhood-scale. *Hedgehog Street* is a project that champions this idea and is looking for volunteers to encourage neighbours to ensure gardens are accessible and that suitable habitats are joined up (see *Further reading*, page 100). Already, thousands of people are taking part.

We share the built environment with predators and browsers, aerial gymnasts and burrowers. Taking the time to record them as part of a survey is invaluable: their habitat is our habitat and 'citizen science' is best placed to better understand it.

Hedgehog Street (www.hedgehogstreet.org)

Appendix 1 – A brief taxonomy

Taxonomy is the classification of organisms into groups that share characteristics. Each group (except for the top one) is put into a larger group: species are collected into genera; genera into families; families into orders; and so on, up a taxonomic hierarchy to kingdom. But similarities tend to run in families and taxonomy does more than put names to specimens in museum drawers: it describes how organisms are related; it helps us to make sense of the diversity of life.

The two-part scientific name (for example *'Mustela erminea'*) is formed from the genus *(Mustela)* and species *(erminea)* names, and is always printed in italics, with a lower-case initial for species. The genus, family and higher group names are written with a capital initial.

Mammals form one distinct group of animals within those that have a backbone. Worldwide, the class Mammalia is made up of 29 large groups, called orders, containing 5,676 species at a recent count. Eight orders occur in Britain or around its coasts (pinnipeds – seals and walruses – are within the group Carnivora, related to mustelids and bears respectively, but have become specialised to an aquatic lifestyle).

Order	Family	Species
Eulipotyphla	Erinaceidae	*Erinaceus europaeus* **hedgehog**
	Talpidae	*Talpa europaea* **mole**
	Soricidae	*Sorex araneus* **common shrew** *Sorex minutus* **pygmy shrew** *Neomys fodiens* **water shrew** *Crocidura suaveolens* lesser white-toothed (Scilly) shrew *Crocidura russula* greater white-toothed shrew
Rodentia	Muridae	*Apodemus sylvaticus* **wood mouse** *Apodemus flavicollis* **yellow-necked mouse** *Mus domesticus* **house mouse** *Micromys minutus* harvest mouse *Rattus rattus* **black rat** *Rattus norvegicus* **brown rat**
	Gliridae	*Muscardinus avellanarius* hazel dormouse *Glis glis* fat dormouse
	Cricetidae	*Myodes glareolus* **bank vole** *Microtus agrestis* **field vole** *Microtus arvalis* Orkney and Guernsey voles *Arvicola amphibious* **water vole**
	Sciuridae	*Sciurus vulgaris* **red squirrel** *Sciurus carolinensis* **grey squirrel**
Lagomorpha	Leporidae	*Oryctolagus cuniculus* **rabbit** *Lepus europaeus* brown hare *Lepus timidus* mountain hare

Carnivora	Canidae	*Vulpes vulpes* **fox**
	Mustelidae	*Meles meles* **badger** *Mustela erminea* **stoat** *Mustela nivalis* **weasel** *Mustela putorius* polecat *Lutra lutra* **otter** *Neovison vison* **mink** *Martes martes* **pine marten**
	Felidae	*Felis silvestris* wildcat
(Pinnipedia)	Phocidae	*Halichoerus grypus* grey seal *Phoca vitulina* common seal
Artiodactyla	Cervidae	*Cervus elaphus* red deer *Cervus nippon* sika *Dama dama* fallow deer *Capreolus capreolus* **roe deer** *Muntiacus reevesi* **Reeves' muntjac** *Hydropotes inermis* Chinese water deer
	Suidae	*Sus scrofa* wild boar
Cetacea	Delphinidae	*Tursiops truncatus* bottlenose dolphin
	Phocoenidae	*Phocoena phocoena* harbour porpoise
	Balaenoptenidae	*Balaenoptera acutorostrata* minke whale
Chiroptera	Vespertilionidae	*Pipistrellus pipistrellus* **common pipistrelle** *Pipistrellus pygmaeus* **soprano pipistrelle** *Pipistrellus nathusii* Nathusius' pipistrelle *Myotis mystacinus* whiskered bat *Myotis brandtii* Brandt's bat *Myotis alcathoe* Alcathoe bat *Myotis nattereri* Natterer's bat *Myotis bechsteinii* Bechstein's bat *Myotis daubentonii* **Daubenton's bat** *Eptesicus serotinus* **serotine** *Nyctalus leisleri* Leisler's bat *Nyctalus noctula* noctule *Barbastella barbastellus* barbastelle *Plecotus auritus* **brown long-eared bat** *Plecotus austriacus* grey long-eared bat
	Rhinolophidae	*Rhinolophus hipposiderus* lesser horseshoe bat *Rhinolophus ferrumequinum* greater horseshoe bat
Diprotodontia	Macropodidae	*Macropus rufogriseus* red-necked wallaby

A checklist of mammals that occur in Britain. The most urbanite species are shown in **bold.**

An evolutionary tree of urban mammals.

A 'family tree' of the mammals found in urban areas in Britain. The tree shows the relationship between species or groups: those on adjacent branches are more closely related to each other than to those on more distant branches. Squirrels, for example, are more closely related to rats and mice than they are to other species, and are put in the same group, the *order* Rodentia. Within groups, *families* are identified such as Muridae (rats and mice), and Mustelidae (the mustelid or weasel family) in the order Carnivora. The relatedness of two species is estimated from similarities in their genes and physical characteristics.

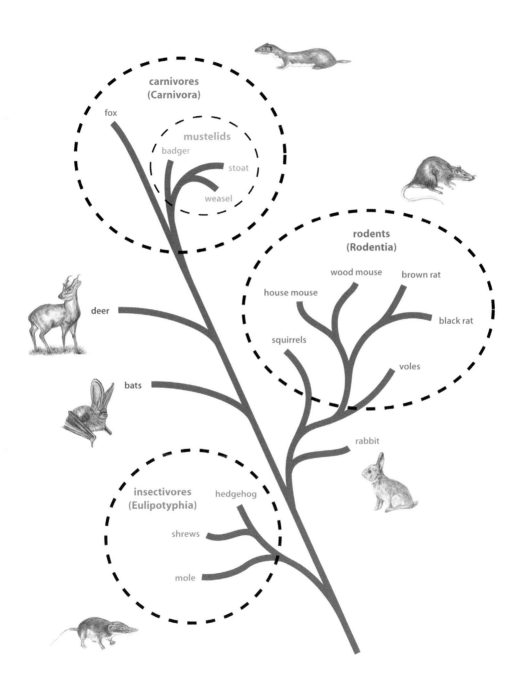

carnivores
(Carnivora)

fox

mustelids

badger

stoat

weasel

rodents
(Rodentia)

wood mouse   brown rat

house mouse

black rat

deer

squirrels

voles

bats

rabbit

insectivores
(Eulipotyphia)   hedgehog

shrews

mole

Appendix 2 – Garden microhabitats

1. **Hedges** provide food and shelter, and – just as importantly – access for many mammals to and from gardens.

2. **Log piles** nurture a multitude of invertebrates – prey for many mammal species – and provide nest sites for wood mice.

3. **Compost heaps**, like log piles, support a diverse community of invertebrates and fungi, mimicking a forest floor.

4. **Ponds** should have a means of escape, such as a wire-mesh 'ladder' or shallow-sided area, and can benefit mammals as watering holes and sources of prey such as invertebrates and amphibians.

5. **Plants** producing berries or seeds, and fruit or vegetable crops, are on the menu of many mammal species.

6. **Leaf piles** provide cover and nest sites, as well as a source of invertebrates.

7. **Trees and tall shrubs** are perhaps the single most important feature of gardens in encouraging small mammals and insects, providing an array of food and microhabitats.

8. **Long grass** provides cover for voles and shrews, and summer nest sites for hedgehogs.

9. **Gaps or small holes** in a fence ensure a garden is accessible: even a very small space, if it joins up with others, can attract mammals and support biodiversity.

Glossary

Arboreal Living or active in trees, e.g. red squirrels and pine martens.

Biodiversity The variety of species and communities in nature, and of genes and populations within species. Green spaces and the biodiversity they support in cities provide benefits such as cleaner air, flood protection and better health.

Buck The adult male of some species, especially rabbits and roe deer.

Carnivorous Describing an animal (or plant) that feeds mainly on other animals.

Carnivora A taxonomic group that includes the dog, cat and mustelid (weasel) families.

Colony A group of organisms of the same species living together or sharing a home.

Commensal Literally 'eating at the same table'; in biology, it describes an association between two species where one benefits and the other is unaffected.

Connectivity The degree to which a landscape helps or hinders movement between habitat patches.

Courtship The behaviour of animals to attract a breeding partner.

Crepuscular Active mainly at dawn and dusk, during twilight.

Diurnal Active mainly during daylight hours.

Doe The adult female of some species, including roe deer, muntjac and rabbits.

Dorsal Belonging to the back of the body.

Drey The nest built by a red or grey squirrel, usually high in the branches of a tall tree.

Earth The den of a fox.

Echolocation A natural sonar used by bats and some other species to orientate themselves and to find prey. The animal listens for echoes of high-pitched calls that bounce off objects, and uses the strength and direction of the sound to build up a picture of its surroundings.

Genus (plural: genera) The taxonomic group above *species*. It forms the first part of the scientific name.

Family The taxonomic group above *genus* and below *order*. The weasel family (Mustelidae), for example, has seven species in Britain, in four genera (*Mustela, Lutra, Neovison* and *Martes*).

Feral Describes domesticated animals that are living in the wild.

Hibernaculum (plural: hibernacula) The sheltered site or nest of an animal, used to overwinter or hibernate in.

Hibernation A dormant state that some animals adopt in winter, when it is cold and food is scarce. Hibernating animals slow their heart rate and metabolism to conserve energy. In Britain, bat species, hedgehogs, and hazel and fat dormice hibernate.

Holt The den of an otter, most often in natural cavities but sometimes in culverts or drain pipes.

Home range The area used by an individual during its normal activities of foraging, finding a mate and caring for offspring.

Insectivorous Describing an animal (or plant) that feeds mainly on insects.

Invertebrate An animal without a backbone, such as insects, earthworms, spiders and snails. Invertebrates form a large part of the diet of many mammals.

Murine Belonging to the rodent family Muridae, which includes mice and rats.

Mustelid A member of the weasel family, Mustelidae. Seven mustelid species occur in Britain: stoats, weasels, badgers, mink, otters, polecats and pine martens, and belong to the order Carnivora.

Native Original to a particular place. 'Native' is often used to describe those species in Britain that were present when Britain became an island, around 11,000 years ago. Non-native mammal species are those that have arrived since, accidently or deliberately introduced by people. A very few new arrivals can become invasive and cause a problem, but many – such as rabbits and brown hares – have become as 'traditional' as native species.

Order The taxonomic group above *family*, e.g. Chiroptera (bats) and Eulipotyphla (shrews, moles and hedgehogs).

Raptor A bird of prey, such as a buzzard or sparrowhawk. Raptors, along with owls, are common predators of small mammals.

Refugia (singular: refugium) Areas that have escaped ecological change, preserving a suitable habitat for a species.

Scat The dropping of some animals, including foxes and pine martens.

Slots The hoof-prints of deer, showing the two toes.

Species A group of organisms that are able to breed with each other (producing offspring that are also able to breed) and forming a more or less contained 'gene pool'.

Spraint The dropping of an otter.

Taxonomy The classification of organisms into groups that share characteristics and a common ancestry. Taxonomic groups (such as *order, genus* and *species*) are arranged in levels, each one containing the groups below it.

Territory An area actively defended by an animal against other individuals of the same species for food or other resources.

Ungulate A hoofed mammal, such as roe deer or muntjac.

Ultrasound Sound whose pitch (frequency) is above that that humans can hear (greater than 20 kHz). Ultrasound can be heard by many mammals and is used by some, such as bats, to echolocate.

UKBAP UK Biodiversity Action Plan. The UK government's response to the 1992 Convention on Biological Diversity, which identified priority species for conservation efforts. New policy has since replaced it.

Ventral Belonging to the front of the body or the side normally facing the ground.

Vertebrate An animal that has a backbone – mammals, birds, reptiles, amphibians and fish.

Further reading

A broader account of British mammal species, including the less urbanite ones, is given in:
Britain's Mammals: a concise guide, People's Trust for Endangered Species (Whittet Books, 2010)

Several titles in Whittet's *British Natural History Series* give informative and readable accounts of individual urban species, including:

The New Hedgehog Book, Pat Morris (Whittet Books, 2006, revised 2010)
Urban Foxes, *Second Edition,* Stephen Harris and Phil Baker (Whittet Books, 2001)
Badgers, Michael Clark (Whittet Books, 2000, revised 2010)
Otters, Paul Chanin, *The British Natural History Collection, Volume 2* (Whittet Books, 2012)

Jennifer Owen's remarkable study of her own garden is detailed in:
Wildlife of a Garden, A Thirty-Year Study, Jennifer Owen (Royal Horticultural Society, 2010)

An inspirational practical guide to encouraging insects into gardens (and in turn mammals) is:
Gardening for Butterflies, Bees and Other Beneficial Insects, Jan Miller-Klein (Saith Ffynnon Books, 2010)

Information about the Biodiversity in Urban Gardens (BUGS) projects, run by the University of Sheffield, can be found at:
http://www.bugs.group.shef.ac.uk/

More information about bats and buildings is available at the Bat Conservation Trust's webpage:
http://www.bats.org.uk/pages/bats_and_buildings.html
and in the Bats and Buildings guidance leaflet:
http://www.bats.org.uk/publications_download.php/247/Bats_and_Buildings_finalDec2010.pdf

A general guide to enhancing buildings for wildlife is published by the Royal Institute of British Architects:
Biodiveristy for Low and Zero Carbon Buildings, Carol William (RIBA Publishing, 2010)

Taking part

Recording observations of wildlife contributes directly to scientific research and conservation. Urban mammals are recorded in:

People's Trust for Endangered Species' *Living with Mammals* survey
http://www.ptes.org/lwm

The British Hedgehog Preservation Society and PTES' *Hedgehog Street* project, which describes how to encourage urban hedgehogs on a neighbourhood-scale
http://www.hedgehogstreet.org

The British Trust for Ornithology's *Garden BirdWatch*
http://www.bto.org/volunteer-surveys/gbw

Index

Acknowledgements

Part of the text is based on sections from *Britain's Mammals: a concise guide* (published by Whittet Books), by David Wembridge and Clare Poland Bowen.

Kelly Gunnell (Bat Conservation Trust) wrote the text for the 'Bats and buildings' section (pages 18-19); Henry Johnson, Philip Briggs (BCT) and Gavin Broad read the whole or drafts of sections and answered questions.

Picture credits (by page):

(Front cover) © Laurent Geslin/naturepl.com. (1) Chris Packham: All Electric Productions, (2) Crowd: ©iStockphoto.com/adisa, (3) Fox: Ian Wade, (4) Garden: David Wembridge, Park: ©iStockphoto.com/oversnap, Allotment: Anita Burrough, (8) Rabbits: Laurie Campbell, (10) Badger: Laurie Campbell, (11) Badger: Dave Bevan, (12) Badger: Laurie Campbell, Badger prints: Anita Burrough, Badger path: Dave Bevan, (13) Brown long-eared bat: Laurie Campbell, (14) Pipistrelle: Laurie Campbell, (15) Sonogram: Bat Conservation Trust, (16) Brown long-eared bat: Hugh Clark/Bat Conservation Trust, (17) Bat droppings: Pat Morris, (18) Brown long-eared bats between rafters: Paul Sutherland, Habitat drawing: EcosurvLtd, (19) Pipistrelle roost in cladding: Ian Birch, Brown long-eared bats in roof void: Hugh Clark (20) Brown rat: Maureen Dinsdale, (21) Brown rat: Laurie Campbell, (22) Rat droppings: Janice Whittingdon, (22) Rat hole: Jill Nelson, (23) Grey squirrel: Laurie Campbell, (24) Grey squirrel: Laurie Campbell, (25) Squirrel drey: Rachel Saunders, Squirrel tracks: Pat Morris, Nuts: Dave Bevan, (26) Red squirrel: Laurie Campbell, (27) Hedgehog: Dave Bevan, (28) Hedgehog: Steve Heliczer, (29) Hedgehog tracks: Ian Gray, Hedgehog dropping: PTES, (30) Wood mouse: Dave Bevan, (31) House mouse: Dave Bevan, (32) Horse chestnut: Laurie Campbell, Mouse droppings: Peter Bagshaw, (33) Wood mouse: Laurie Campbell, (34) Nuts: Dave Bevan, Mouse nest: Dave Bevan, (35) Mole: Laurie Campbell, (36) Mole: Dave Bevan, (37) Mole hills: Dave Bevan, Mole tunnel: Martyn L. Gorman, (38) Rabbit: Laurie Campbell, (39) Rabbit: Laurie Campbell, (40) Rabbit droppings: Pat Morris, Rabbit holes: Pat Morris, Rabbit tracks: Pat Morris, (41) Fox: Colin Mackenzie, (42) Fox cubs: PTES, (43) Fox print: Rachel Saunders, Fox scat: PTES, (44) Bank vole: Dave Bevan, (45) Bank vole: Pat Morris. (46) Nut: PTES, Chewed grass outside vole burrow: Laurie Campbell, (47) Water vole eating meadowsweet leaves: Laurie Campbell, (48) Weasel: Stephen Oliver, (50) Roe deer: Laurie Campbell, (51) Muntjac: Dave Bevan, Small muntjac images: Alison Burton, (52) Muntjac: Laurie Campbell, Muntjac droppings: Pat Morris, (53) Roe deer: Laurie Campbell, (54) Roe deer droppings: Pat Morris, (55) Otter: Laurie Campbell, (56) Otter: Laurie Campbell, (57) Otter spraints: Laurie Campbell, Holt: Laurie Campbell, Otter prints: Laurie Campbell, (58) Pine marten: Declan O'Mahony, (59) Pine marten: Laurie Campbell, (60) Cottage: Declan O'Mahony, Pine marten sprint: Declan O'Mahony, (61) Red squirrel: Dave Bevan, (62) Bark: Laurie Campbell, Red squirrel prints: Laurie Campbell, (63) Pygmy shrew: Dave Bevan, (64) Pygmy shrew: Dave Bevan, (65) Barn owl pellet: Andrew Waller, (66) Water shrew: Pat Morris, (67) Water shrew: Pat Morris, (68) Pygmy shrew: Dave Bevan, (69) Stoat: Laurie Campbell, (70) Stoat: Laurie Campbell, (71) Stoat scat: www.talesfromthewood.com, Stoat kill: www.talesfromthewood.com, (72) Weasel: Stephen Oliver, (73) Weasel: Laurie Campbell, (74) Yellow-necked mouse: Dave Bevan, (75) Nest: Dave Bevan, (76) Houses: ©iStockphoto.com/Anthony Brown, (77) Hawthorn: PTES, (78) Rat-tail plantain: Roger Key, (79) Illustration: PTES, Compost heap: David Wembridge, (80) Cat: David Wembridge, Hedgehog: Simon Oldfield, (82) Mole tunnel system diagram: Martyn L. Gorman, (83) Foxgloves: PTES, Lavender: ©iStockphoto.com/Peter Clark, Berberis: ©iStockphoto.com/Rachel Dunn, (84) Badger: Laurie Campbell, (87) Bat: Laurie Campbell, (Back cover) Hedgehog: Dave Bevan, Fox: ©iStockphoto.com/Benny Rytter, Brown rat: Maureen Dinsdale, Chris Packham: All Electric Productions.

Weasel/stoat illustration (page 73) and family tree illustrations (page 95): Amy Whetstone, Wood/yellow-necked mouse illustration (page 74): Susan Sharafi, Garden illustration (page 97): Vanessa Wembridge.

Distribution maps: based on material supplied by Midsummer Books Ltd and Bright Star Publishing Ltd from *Wildlife of Britain*, © Midsummer Books Ltd and Bright Star Publishing Ltd.

About the People's Trust for Endangered Species

Established for over 30 years, the People's Trust for Endangered Species is a conservation charity working worldwide to ensure a future for endangered species. Our varied and extensive work ranges from direct support for conservationists to involving the public and volunteers in practical action to help specific species and their habitats. We have a special interest in protecting Britain's wild mammals. We run wildlife events for people to enjoy our sometimes elusive wild mammals in their natural habitats and we involve thousands of people nationwide in monitoring how they are doing. By purchasing this book and by becoming a regular supporter you will have the satisfaction of knowing that you are supporting our work and really making a difference to conservation on your doorstep. Thank you.

Jill Nelson
Chief Executive

www.ptes.org

Also from PTES

Britain's Mammals
a concise guide

The essential illustrated guide to the mammals found in Britain and around its coast, along with some that are now extinct.

'This family-friendly book is packed full of fascinating facts about more than 60 species, covering diet, habitat, predators, reproduction and conservation status, and with an evolutionary family tree and track-identification chart, *Britain's Mammals* is great value for money.'
BBC Wildlife magazine

'The species pages are a rich delight to read. The guide packs into each page an admirable range of information, all very clearly displayed, with a consistency that encourages and facilitates comparison. *Britain's Mammals* is a fascinating and well-crafted volume, with a refreshingly crisp and contemporary interpretation of its subject … This book cannot fail to prove useful and interesting to any reader with the slightest interest in Britain's mammals, and is strongly recommended.'
The Ranger's Blog, Naturenet

'This is essentially an introduction to the mammals of the UK and it is much more than an illustrated guide as it can also claim to be an up-to-date reference … One only has to think of the various deer species, mink, otter and mountain hare to realise the importance of up-to-date information. This is a book I have already consulted, as few others have current information about the species … The publishers and authors should be congratulated on this boost to the conservation of mammals at a time when many of them are in dire straits.'
Ray Collier, Highland News

'The ideal introduction to the subject, but just as valuable to the older generation of naturalists like me who easily get out of date.'
Michael Clark, Country-Side (the magazine of the British Naturalists' Association)

'Great book, beautifully produced.'
Laurie Campbell, wildlife photographer

Published by Whittet Books, ISBN 978 1 873580 81 3